H. H. Stuckenschmidt

Twentieth Century Music

Translated from the German
by Richard Deveson

World University Library

Weidenfeld and Nicolson
5 Winsley Street London W1

Für Hilde und Heinrich Strobel, eingedenk
guter und böser Jahre.

© H. H. Stuckenschmidt 1969
Translation © George Weidenfeld and Nicolson Ltd 1969
Phototypeset by BAS Printers Limited, Wallop, Hampshire
Printed by Officine Grafiche Arnoldo Mondadori, Verona

Contents

Acknowledgments

Acknowledgment – further to any made in the captions – is due to the following for illustrations (the number refers to the page on which the illustration appears):
9 Victoria and Albert Museum, London; 10 Donald Southern (Covent Garden Opera); 12 Boosey and Hawkes Ltd; 15 Westminster Public Libraries; 18, 126, 130 Novosti Press Agency; 23 Mansell Collection; 27 Mr Richard Buckle; 37 Mr Peter Williams; 43 Miss Rosamund Ley; 53 Mr Lawrence Schoenberg; 59 Houston Rogers (Covent Garden Opera); 61 Mr John Russell; 69, 169 United States Information Service; 76 M. André Meyer, Mme Tcherkessov and Mr Richard Buckle; 78, 184 Camera Press Ltd; 99, 171 Libraire Stock; 110, 129 Reg Wilson (Covent Garden Opera); 117 Keystone Press Agency; 121 Ullstein Bilderdienst; 139 Mr Jack Phipps; 143, 219 Evan Senior; 146 INGI; 152 Royal College of Music; 158 Hungarian News and Information Service; 160 Paul Popper Ltd; 188–9 Professor Lejaren A. Hiller and the Champaign Urbana News Gazette; 196 Radio Times Hulton Picture Library; 215 Lotte Meitner-Graf; 221 Edward Piper; 222 Universal Edition Ltd; 227, 237 Italian Institute, London; 240, 243 Central Press Agency (CAF), Warsaw.

Two music extracts in this book have been reproduced direct from score, by permission of (for Stockhausen, 200–1) Universal Edition (London) Ltd, and (for Cage, 230–1) Edition Peters (Copyright 1960 by C. F. Peters Corp., New York). Other musical illustrations have been based on scores published by the following: Universal Edition Ltd (for Schoenberg 33, 62 [*Pierrot Lunaire*], 93 [with Schott], 163; for Hába 42; for Webern 56–7; for Berg 58, 164; for Stockhausen 66; for Bennett 165). Durand et Cie (for Ravel 36; for Debussy 66; for Messiaen 166–7). Boosey and Hawkes Ltd (for Bartók 35). Edition Russe de Musique (for Stravinsky 38). Schirmer (for Schoenberg [*Ode to Napoleon*] 62). Schott (for Cowell 66; for Schoenberg 93 [with Universal Edition]). Suvini Zerboni (for Bartók 75). Bomart Music Publications Inc. (for Ives 83). J. and W. Chester Ltd (for Stravinsky 84).

All the music was chosen, arranged where necessary, and written by Tim Souster. The diagrams on pages 50–1 and 56–7 were drawn by Trevor Vincent.

The diagram on pages 50–1 is based on a figure in W. H. Thorpe, *Bird Song* (Cambridge University Press, 1961).

1 Romanticism and anti-romanticism

Art in the second half of the nineteenth century bears the heavy burden of the Romantic Agony. The pathos and *Weltschmerz* of Berlioz and Byron was intensified in the philosophy of Wagner and became a cult of suffering finding sanctuary in the idea of redemption. Art had long been a purely subjective means of expression, and the surplus in emotion had long since overrun the frontiers of traditional forms. Wagner was in this sense not merely the great theoretician of the romantic striving for infinity, but the creator of an artistic view of life which knew no rules that cannot be overthrown. The art of the late romantic period can trace its hostility to life back to the worlds of suffering of *Tristan* and of Amfortas in *Parsifal*. This is true not of music alone but of a significant part of the literature of the *fin de siècle*, drama in particular. The immensity of Wagner's European influence is demonstrated by the poetry of Baudelaire and Verlaine and by the novels and plays of Strindberg. Not merely agony, but the ability to give expression to it in its most intensified form, became the paramount aim in the aesthetic hierarchy of the age. Novelists such as Thomas Mann and Proust cultivated this strange pleasure in sickness and disease and exhibited it in works of the highest quality.

Whenever music takes on the task of expression, it develops new technical means. Emotional music cannot remain satisfied with well-worn classical elements of construction which have been reduced to mere formulae. In romantic music this urge to create new sounds was stronger than in any previous cultural epoch. The extent to which new harmonic and melodic techniques were developed from the time of the romantic *Lied* of Franz Schubert to the early works of Schoenberg exceeded the achievements of the whole period between 1600 and 1800. In an art-form intent on intimacy and subtlety of expression each smallest cell and element in the individual work of art needs to be determined. Like romantic lyric poetry, romantic harmony is an art of nuances, of minute ramifications and transitions. When it uses the technique of variation, whether in the rhyme of Mallarmé or the *Leitmotiv* of Wagner, deviations from the thematic idea are minimal. The smallest reverberations in feeling are matched by the smallest modifications in the work of art. This gives rise to the paradox that an excess pressure of emotion seeks and finds its outlet in the most delicate arteries of an artistic organism whose *raison d'être* is emotion itself. There indeed lies the distinction between the pathos of romanticism and the *Weltschmerz* of Goethe's *Werther*, which, while accepting the inevitability of suicide, yet, by virtue of the difference in artistic means, stops short at a point dictated by the classical sense of form.

A further contradictory feature of this view of art is the contrast between intimacy of expression and formal expansion. Beethoven and Schubert had already imposed massive dimensions on the classical sonata and symphony, and they were themselves superseded by Berlioz, Schumann and Liszt. Wagner went furthest of all in the *Ring*. A great cycle of novels such as Zola's Rougon-Macquart series is unmistakably related to the great musical cycles of the nineteenth century. Even the epic sagas of Romain Rolland and Proust show this Wagnerian desire for infinity (*Unendlichkeit*) or for the portrayal of a miniature cosmos. In the purely musical sphere, the nine symphonies of Bruckner are a similar expression of cosmic and cyclic thought and creation. Indeed, in Bruckner the principle of variation can be seen on a gigantically expanded scale. Each of his symphonies is in a sense a new variant of one and the same type, which was itself sketched out in the earlier works and exists fully developed from the fourth symphony on.

Attempts have been made to explain the odd romantic contradiction between intimacy and vastness by reference to the scientific and social developments of the nineteenth century. The growth of mechanisation and industrialisation at the beginning of the romantic era did indeed encourage both tendencies. Scientific thought, in accordance with the modern research methods developed after 1800, proceeds by observation of the smallest cells and units. The microscope is the symbol of this style of thought. It opened up a world of micro-organisms, very much as chromatic harmony unfolded a world of tiny nuances of sound. At the same time, the industrial production of goods created orders of magnitude which far out-

The vague longings and fluidity of form of Wagner's
Rhinemaidens (here painted by F. Matania) symbolise
the composer's romantic drama style. Perhaps, too, they
express the over-chromaticism of music generally
at the end of the nineteenth century, when fluidity of
harmonic relationships could go no further.

Strauss's *Elektra*: the composer recoiled from the dark world that his early (1908) disregard for tonality opened up.

stripped all earlier ones. The speed with which ships and trains could cover distances encouraged men to think in far greater geographical units. The newly-emergent middle class made unlimited use of these possibilities and experiences. And it was the spirit of this very middle class, the product of a scientific and industrial age, which found its expression in the art of the nineteenth century.

A new generation of composers came forward in the eighties whose sensibility was conditioned in the same way by Wagner's oeuvre and musical language. They too sought a more intense form of expression by using new techniques, larger-scale forms, and working with small units or motifs. In the German-speaking world the foremost representatives of this generation were Richard Strauss and Gustav Mahler. Dissimilar as the two were in intellectual make-up and personality, and despite their use of very different forms, their music evokes similar responses. Their musical styles exhibit common features, uniting Wagnerian techniques and a chamber-music style derived from Brahms.

In his early symphonic poems, *Macbeth*, *Don Juan*, *Till Eulenspiegel* and *Ein Heldenleben*, Strauss continued the tradition of Franz Liszt. He expanded the sphere of chromatic harmony so as to fuse two or three tonalities, and widened the scope of the orchestral colour so that instruments lost their individual autonomy. His late-romantic *Weltschmerz*, present even in *Don Juan*, was matched from the first by a youthful optimism very similar to that prevalent in the new German Empire of 1871.

Strauss's first music-drama, *Guntram*, followed the pattern of the Wagnerian opera of redemption. Yet his next work, *Feuersnot* (1901), was a burlesque, composed to words by Ernst von Wolzogen, the founder of the German literary cabaret, the Buntes Theater. In the music-dramas *Salome* (1905) and *Elektra* (1909) Strauss developed Wagner's expressive style into something verging on later expressionism, and achieved at the same time a radical abbreviation and compression of both form and content. The harmonic language of both works, with its use of cumulative unresolved dissonances, often extends beyond the bounds of tonality, and the vocal line assumes at times the character of impassioned outbursts and cries.

After *Elektra*, Strauss felt he could no longer continue on the same course, and he abandoned it. The calmer language of *Der Rosenkavalier* is the first instance in post-Wagnerian music of a regressive tendency that we shall observe in the works of several composers of disparate kinds. This turning-point in Strauss's creative career came to light with the first performance of *Der*

Mahler (1860–1911) spent his public musical life in opera and theatre but wrote nothing for the stage. His enormous symphonies are likewise personal statements. But his musical language, extremely chromatic, is the starting-point for Schoenberg's rejection of harmonic relations and his own personality with its alternations of naive joy and haunted fears symbolises both the state of music and of mankind itself on the brink of the modern era.

Rosenkavalier at Dresden in 1911. The world-wide success of the work justified him. In *Ariadne auf Naxos*, which soon followed (1912, revised 1916), Strauss again showed a tendency towards simplification, reducing his orchestra to chamber proportions. Yet on later occasions he reverted to the more difficult and complicated style of *Salome* and *Elektra*, as in *Die Frau ohne Schatten* (1919) and *Die Ägyptische Helena* (1928). After the preliminary autobiographical essay, *Intermezzo* (1925), he perfected a highly refined *buffo* style, which was notably successful in *Arabella* (1933), *Die schweigsame Frau* (1935), and *Capriccio* (1942). Strauss's whole career as an operatic composer was crucially affected by his meeting with the Austrian poet Hugo von Hofmannsthal. While *Elektra* had been a setting of a text originally written as a play (as *Salome* had been of Oscar Wilde's original), the later works from *Der Rosenkavalier* to *Arabella* were settings of genuine original libretti. The Hofmannsthal-Strauss collaboration, which ended in 1929 with Hofmannsthal's death, was interrupted only once. This was during the First World War, when Strauss started work on his own text of *Intermezzo*. The composition took him until 1923 and was thus itself interrupted by the completion of *Die Frau ohne Schatten*.

Strauss made some important contributions to the thoroughgoing renewal of music. He rose from the Bavarian *haute bourgeoisie* to become a sophisticated man of the world. He personified better than any of his musical contemporaries the spirit of positivism and progress. The idyllic, romantic world of his songs was shattered by the forcefulness of his musico-dramatic language. Having extended Wagnerian pathos to its limits, he replaced it by a relaxed, virtuosic, comic style. His native optimism grew darker with scepticism and experience. The triumphant gesture he could command so well often gave way to a feeling of resignation, as in the moving and valedictory *Metamorphosen* (1946) for twenty-three solo strings.

Gustav Mahler, born four years before Strauss in 1860, came from a Jewish provincial background in Moravia. Like Strauss, he trained as an operatic conductor and from 1885 to 1911 was one of the great conductors of the time. Although connected with opera

A detail from the autograph score of Mahler's *Tenth Symphony*. The marginal comments read 'Have mercy!', 'O God, why hast thou forsaken me?'.

from his youth, and a leading spirit in the theatre in Prague, Budapest, Hamburg and Vienna, he composed nothing for the stage, devoting his creative work almost exclusively to the *Lied* and the symphony. In the *Lieder eines fahrenden Gesellen* he achieved a folk-song style of the kind that post-Wagnerian music had un-learned. The songs are primarily an expression of effusive and rap-turous feelings: unrestrained surrender to joy and sorrow, love of nature, bucolic humour, as well as an occasional sense of horror and a hint of daemonic forces. Mahler composed the songs under the impact of a great and unhappy love affair. He wrote to a friend in 1884:

The songs are conceived as a whole: you must imagine a journeyman apprentice who has had a fateful experience and now goes out into the world and travels on alone.

And later:

My Sphinx never ceases to stare and cast riddles in my face – for the rest, I am treated as a half-wit . . . people are partly well-meaning and sympathetic, partly gloating and curious.

Mahler's First Symphony has close thematic links with the song-cycle. It was completed in 1888, at the same time as Strauss's *Macbeth*. The work has the dimensions of the symphonies of Anton Bruckner, under whom Mahler had studied in Vienna. The four-movement form and the use of a large orchestra are a further reminder of Bruckner. Yet Mahler's folk-song style is still recog-nisable in the themes of this purely instrumental work. The great singing line that characterises the instrumentation and the poly-phonic textures denotes a form of musical thinking quite different from that which we saw in Strauss. It is a highly distinctive feature that remained unchanged in all the tempestuous development Mahler underwent in his symphonies and songs. His was the most deeply-stirred sensibility of the musicians of his generation. His romantic intensity of feeling becomes so heightened that it bursts the bonds of human and earthly experience.

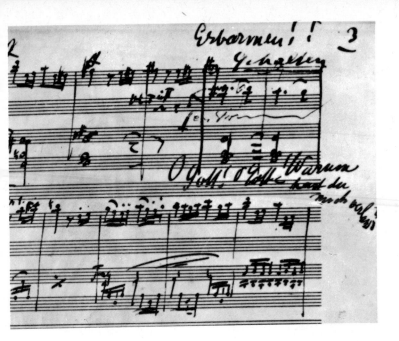

Mahler's music has at times an almost medieval mystical yearning for God; in general it knows only the extremes of rejoicing and profound depression. Now and then a world of ghosts and grimaces emerges between the extremes: in the grotesque scherzi and marches, the visions of spirits, and the weird outbursts which sound like echoes from the primary world of agony. Mahler takes the development of techniques even further than Strauss; he outdoes even Bruckner in the expansion of symphonic form. His Eighth Symphony, composed in 1907 but not performed until 1910, lasts ninety minutes and because of the massive forces involved has become known as the 'Symphony of a Thousand'. As in the Second Symphony (1894), the Third (1896) and the Fourth (1900), Mahler employs solo voices and chorus in addition to a large orchestra. The medieval hymn *Veni creator spiritus* and the final scene from Part Two of Goethe's *Faust* are his text. A further important work in Mahler's oeuvre is *Das Lied von der Erde* of 1908. It is a song-cycle based on Chinese poems with additional verses of the composer's own. Although not a symphony as such, it attains a degree of motivic and harmonic unity that is found only sporadically in the symphonies of Beethoven and Schumann.

In his last works, the Ninth Symphony and the unfinished Tenth, Mahler's drive towards an ever more intense self-expression led him to a yet further expansion of techniques. The melodic writing traverses huge intervals, and the harmony generates towering chords of ten and eleven notes. These are purely instrumental symphonies, without text. Yet the written comments in the manuscript scores of both bear heart-rending testimony to the tragic experiences Mahler suffered while composing them. With Strauss, who did not share his metaphysical attitude to life, Mahler prepared a later generation for the experience of expressionism.

In Russia at this time, quite independently of these German composers, the figure of Alexander Scriabin came to the fore. He belonged to the intellectual circle of Sergei Taneiev, himself a pupil of Tchaikovsky and Nicolai Rubinstein. Scriabin was an outstanding pianist and he wrote predominantly piano music. His earlier models were Liszt, and Chopin from whom he inherited a highly refined harmonic and melodic sense and a penchant for small, compressed forms. He had a natural tendency to heighten the expression of emotion, which was reinforced by his Russian temperament. Scriabin belonged to the Russian modernist movements that were inspired by the French literature of the *fin de siècle*. His passionate interest in Wagner, which developed later, also seems to have been promoted through this French connection. By now the circle of influences had grown: Scriabin's field of vision includes Richard Strauss, and, later and to an even greater degree, Debussy and Ravel. He spent considerable time abroad on concert tours and became familiar with various branches of modern thought. In 1908 he moved to Brussels for three years. Here he came in contact with theosophical circles, and this confirmed his long-standing disposition towards mysticism.

There were two contradictory features in Scriabin's nature. On the one hand he inclined towards an altruistic and compassionate brand of socialism: while in Switzerland he became an irregular supporter of Marxist and revolutionary doctrines. On the other hand he was an out-and-out artistic aristocrat who rejected all forms of popular or national music. In his later life Scriabin sought to realise an ideal of total personal freedom, including sexual relations. His period in Brussels also saw him achieve his most distinctive musical style. What his earlier music had hinted at, the late piano and orchestral pieces now fulfilled. The works reject tonality and the pull of the tonic, and triadic harmony is supplanted by the use of a six-note chord consisting of perfect and altered fourths:

The chord completely dominates the *Promethée* Symphony of 1911 and is also used in subsequent works, such as the Seventh Piano Sonata. By whatever intuition this mystical chord may have been discovered, it is quite open to rational analysis. It uses the eighth, ninth, tenth, eleventh, thirteenth and fourteenth partials in the overtone series, distributed over more than two octaves.

Scriabin's creative ambivalence, his mixture of scientific thinking and speculative fantasy, is characteristic. Like many Romantics of of the early nineteenth century, he tried to co-ordinate the functions of the different sense-organs and thereby of the different arts. He saw quite definite affinities between hearing and seeing, and visualised a *Gesamtkunstwerk*, a 'total' work of art involving both eye and ear but bearing little relation to that of Wagner. A performance of the *Promethée* Symphony (sub-titled *Poème du Feu*) calls for the projection of coloured lights, the colours of which Scriabin lists in a table against given chords. In this respect he was proceeding along a path which was being followed, quite independently, by Kandinsky and Schoenberg in the experimental music-dramas *Der gelbe Klang* and *Die glückliche Hand*. This path was to

Scriabin (1872–1915), mystic, freelance socialist, harmonic innovator and piano-obsessed like Liszt and Chopin, was both completely Russian and yet cosmopolitan in inspiration. His influence was enormous. Pasternak almost gave up a literary for a musical career while under his spell; the young Soviet composers Shostakovich and Prokofiev found their own feet in rebelling against him. In Scriabin's *Promethée*, pitch (in the form of the so-called circle of fifths) is related to the colour spectrum as follows: C – red; G – orange; D – brilliant yellow; A – green; E – blüish-white; B – as E; F sharp – bright blue; D flat – violet; A flat – purple-violet; E flat – steel colour with a metallic lustre; B flat – as E flat; F – red. Here the colour scheme seems to have determined the music's bass-line.

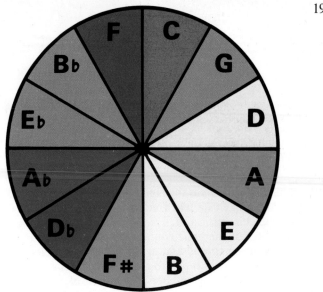

lead from the Romantic realism of Wagner to an increasing abstractness of the artistic material which hinted at future developments.

Scriabin's whole aesthetic is filled with metaphysical and pantheistic notions. This is shown by his *Promethean Fantasies*, a commentary on a work which he planned but never completed owing to his premature death in 1915. He called the work *Mysterium* and envisaged its performance as a kind of mass dance of ecstasy in which the audience would become participants. The entire work was to be a symphony of light, colour, scents and physical contact. As his friend Oskar von Rieseman put it, Scriabin

sought to bring the workings of Nature herself ... into the liturgical, artistic rite of *Mysterium*: the rustling of the trees, the twinkling of the stars, the colours of the rising and setting sun.

Scriabin's *Mysterium* is the high point of late-romantic hyperbole. Scriabin himself felt he had rounded off an epoch with the work. Yet, although his music and personality had a strong influence, they also provoked an energetic counter-reaction. The younger generation of Russians, exposed and in some cases succumbing to a force of this magnitude, was quick to rebel. Musicians such as Prokofiev and Shostakovich found a positive source of inspiration in this rebellion, both in their views of art and in their works.

In Germany Scriabin's music founded no specific school, though it received some attention from the critics. But the circle of Russian artists who formed a small colony in Munich before the First World War took up his ideas with enthusiasm. Kandinsky came to Munich in 1909. With Alexei Yawlensky and Mariana Werefkin he founded the *Neue Künstlervereinigung* from which the *Blaue Reiter* later sprang. The young pianist, composer and writer Thomas von Hartmann also joined this group. He was a supporter of Scriabin and collaborated with Kandinsky as composer in *Der gelbe Klang*. When the famous catalogue of the *Blaue Reiter* appeared in 1912, it contained, besides other contributions on music, an essay by Hartmann on anarchy in music and an article by Leonid Sabaniev on Scriabin's *Promethée*. The same volume also included compositions by Schoenberg and his pupils, Berg and Webern.

Though Mahler and Scriabin differed greatly in intellectual outlook and musical ancestry, common tendencies can be found in their works. Both wished to use the apparatus of the symphony to express metaphysical ideas. Mahler employed a chorus and solo voices to this end (as Beethoven had done before him). Scriabin incorporated the projection of lights in *Promethée*, and for *Mysterium* he planned a gigantic ensemble of instruments and voices with a lavishness recalling Mahler's 'Symphony of a Thousand'. The harmony of both Mahler and Scriabin was a refinement and intensification of the chromaticism of *Tristan* and the *Ring*. Indeed, in Mahler's last symphonies the customary folk-like melodic writing is replaced by an expressionistic thematic style which at times comes close to the excessive thematic wealth of late Scriabin. Taken together, the two composers mark the final stage in the development of romanticism. Yet both inspired a trend which was to run quite contrary to romantic hyperbole.

From the start the opponents of Wagner viewed this over-sophistication and pathos with suspicion. The dominating figure of Wagner was itself enough to crush most opposition, but his critics, and the critics of late romanticism generally, remained alert. They already had a spokesman in Eduard Hanslick, the highly-cultivated music critic and theorist from Prague. He campaigned in Vienna for a kind of artistic counter-reformation and rightly saw its most powerful expression in the music of Brahms. Hanslick's famous essay *On Beauty in Music* had defended 'absolute' music against the claims of the programmatic style as early as 1854. His ideas held their own, particularly in Germany and Austria, and were in fact taken over and given a radical twist by Stravinsky in his Harvard lectures of the thirties. The counter-reaction took further new forms in countries which had not been immediately exposed to the German influence, or had strongly resisted it. In Bohemia and Moravia the Wagner-Liszt school was virtually all-powerful and had thoroughly conditioned the music of great composers such as Smetana and the early Dvořák. But one composer remained completely untouched by it: Leos Janaček, born in 1854. Even his early operas, among them the masterpiece *Jenufa*, are quite different from the *Gesamtkunstwerke* of Wagner and the one-act operas of Strauss. Noble exalted characters are replaced by simple human beings, lifted from the commonplace only by their tragic fate. For all its passion, Janaček's musical language is never forced to an emotional extreme. It has connections with folk-melodies and is based on a quite individual brand of naturalism taken directly from ordinary

language. Janaček succeeded even better than Puccini and the Italian *verismo* composers in writing music comparable with the great Russian, Scandinavian and French literature of the age. His orchestral and choral works share this independence of Wagner and constitute a powerful reaction from the hyper-romanticism and metaphysics of Russian and Austrian music.

In France, Wagner's influence was as widespread as in central Europe. Almost every poet and writer from the 1860s onwards succumbed: Baudelaire, Mallarmé, Gautier, Verlaine. The young composers who were born in the period around 1860 regarded

Debussy did not like to be called an 'impressionist', but his technique does at times resemble that of French painters. Pointillist laws of contrast and analysis, seen in Seurat's 'Le Pont de Courbevoie' (*left*), are also echoed in Debussy's music. Painting in the Courtauld Institute, London.

From Act 1 of Wagner's *Tristan*.
Parallel sevenths are shown in red.
In Debussy's *Pelléas et Mélisande*, the
parallel ninths are similarly marked.

Wagner as a fateful and ineluctable figure with whom they had to come to terms. Even a composer as quintessentially French as Bizet could not escape this completely. Debussy in his youth was a committed Wagnerian. He shocked his fellow-pupils and teachers at the Paris Conservatoire by his radical utopianism. Wagner signified for him the beginning of a new era in which there would be an end to harmonic and tonal tradition. Debussy's harmonies of parallel sevenths and ninths retain their Wagnerian accents even after his attachment to the idol of his youth had completely disappeared. Yet two crucial factors kept the French from complete submission. First, all French art of the period was marked by a growing cultivation of delicacy and restraint. It maintained an aristocratic attitude towards musical expression which proscribed any over-direct or even loud gesture. This was the intellectual basis from which Debussy proceeded, even in his early works, the *Prélude a l'après-midi d'un faune* in particular. Secondly, French music had always kept alive the tradition of a 'modal' melodic and harmonic style, even in the romantic escapades of Berlioz. This ruled out the ever-growing chromaticism that had dominated German music since Bach and, particularly, since *Tristan*. Debussy's use of parallel chord movement is modal to the same degree that Reger's and Strauss's harmony is chromatic. Debussy visited the Bayreuth Festival in 1888 and 89 and soon came to realise the need for a musical language opposed to the romantic pathos of Wagner. He became the spokesman of the anti-Wagnerians. His opera *Pelléas et Mélisande*, based on the play by Maurice Maeterlinck, was composed between 1892 and 1902 and is a fully-fledged example of the new style. It exhibits an introverted form of pathos, a conscious use of understatement, and seeks to express the maximum of emotion with the minimum of musical upheaval. The harmony is no longer functional in the traditional, tonal manner. Sound-phenomena are used in a purely static fashion. Short melodic cells are combined to form a novel motivic language. The use of the whole-tone scale dispels the feeling of a tonal centre; polymetric and polyrhythmic procedures supplant the traditional sense of time and rhythm. Furthermore,

O zah- -me Kunst der Zau- -be-rin

die nur Bal- -sam- trän- ke noch braut!

this is music which does without the explosive, dissonant brutality
of Strauss's scores of the same period. It emphasises the affinities
between chords rather than the differences. The use of multi-
relational seventh and ninth chords, diminished and augmented
triads and four-part chords, gives rise to a kind of harmonic
promiscuity.

Debussy's music has been called impressionistic, although it
came much later than the main body of impressionist painting.
Nevertheless, the two are undoubtedly related: indeed, similarity
to the pointillism of Signac and Seurat is even closer. Furthermore
Debussy, anticipating Scriabin, developed his harmony both by

Parade, Cocteau's ballet to music
by Satie, was produced at the Paris
Théâtre des Champs-Élysées in 1917.
Scenery and costumes were by Picasso.

intuitively pursuing new sensations and by consciously exploiting the higher overtones. Like the theoreticians of impressionism and pointillism, he used scientific data to procure new means of expression. The titles of his piano pieces, particularly the two books of *Préludes* of 1910 and 1913, also show how close he stood to painting and graphic art. Names such as *Les sons et les parfums tournent dans l'air du soir*, *La cathédrale engloutie*, *Brouillards* or *Feux d'artifice* might equally well be attached to impressionist paintings as to pieces of music. The same holds true of his orchestral music. While working on *Pelléas* he wrote the three *Nocturnes* of which the last, *Sirènes*, uses a choir. Between 1903 and 1905 he completed his chief orchestral work, *La Mer;* between 1906 and 1912 he wrote the *Images* for orchestra, among them the 'landscape' *Ibéria*, with its evocations of streets and pathways (*Par les rues and par les chemins*), the perfumes of the night (*Les parfums de la nuit*), and a fiesta morning (*Le matin d'un jour de fête*).

Debussy's music arouses associations and opens up deep-lying levels of consciousness which were necessarily inaccessible to the composers of the high Romantic period. Its restricted dynamics, ranging from *mezzo forte* to quadruple *pianissimo*, produce a kind of musical microcosm built on the most finely-graduated scale. Unlike the expansionism of the post-Wagnerian era in Germany, it is an art of intensity and introversion which heralded a new epoch in musical theory and technique. Debussy's whole development is an impressive and dramatic battle against the dominant idol of his youth, whom he had to overthrow before he could become fully self-sufficient.

Satie and Ravel were luckier in this respect. Satie's earliest works show that he was fully immune to Wagnerian romanticism. Even the chords built on fourths in his music for the play *Le Fils des étoiles* have no links with *Tristan* or *Parsifal*, although the author of the play, Josephe Pelladan, was an enthusiastic Wagnerian (and had also brought Satie into contact with Rosicrucianism). Satie's subsequent 'bare-bone' style—his *musique depouillée*—as displayed in the mocking two-part piano pieces with their ironic titles and inter-

polations, gives no hint that the French intelligentsia had once been bewitched by Wagnerian romanticism. Satie's work is also strikingly related to the ancient modal past, to the scales of Greece and the early church. His preference for popular music and modern American dance rhythms is an unmistakably anti-romantic trait, as witness the *Ragtime du paquebot* from the ballet *Parade*. *Parade* was written during the First World War, in collaboration with Cocteau and with sets and costumes by Picasso, and was produced by Diaghilev's Russian ballet at the Châtelet Theatre in Paris. The work caused a great uproar but made a lasting impression on the younger generation of French musicians. We will have more to say on the effects of Satie's aesthetic views elsewhere. Satie and Debussy were friends for thirty years, ever since their meeting as young men in the Auberge du Olou where Satie was the regular pianist. Satie's anti-Wagnerian views undoubtedly influenced Debussy. This did not prevent Satie from pronouncing a solemn curse on a critic who, in his opinion, had presumptuously found fault with Wagner.

Ravel's case is more complicated. As a very young man he had experienced Wagner's magic in the same way as Debussy, but this had left no trace in his work. In his maturity he dealt with the problem of Wagner's influence on France from a critical point of view, notably in an essay on D'Indy's opera *Fervaal*.

But as a composer, Ravel was immeasurably more receptive to Russian, oriental and other music than he was to German or Austrian influences. Exotic folk-elements found a ready welcome in his musical thought, whether sublimated as in Borodin and Mussorgsky, or in their primal form as shown by the North African and Asiatic musicians at the Paris Exhibition of 1889. Ravel fully integrates such elements into his own musical language: in this respect even his early works display an astonishing degree of individuality and virtuosity. This is shown by his *Shéhérazade* songs and the *Chansons madécasses*, with their rich, exotic flavour, by the Spanish idiom of his *Habañera* and *Alborada del gracioso*, and by the masterly assimilations of Spanish, Greek, Italian and Hebrew folk-music. His virtuosity in mimicry is shown in the piano pieces *à la manière de Borodin et Chabrier*. These stylistic virtues are deeply rooted in the French character, but they exclude the highest forms of romantic expression. In Ravel, as in Rameau in the eighteenth century, they are linked with a characteristically Latin brand of irony. This irony is different from Satie's mockery, which was probably in part attributable to his Irish ancestry. Ravel's luxuriant, voluptuous impressionistic orchestration, as shown in the *Rapsodie espagnole* (1907), the ballet *Daphnis et Chloé* (1909–12), *La Valse* (1919–20), and *Bolero* (1927), is quite different from the instrumentation of Wagner's successors, with their emotional woodwind and brass and *espressivo* strings. His orchestration of Mussorgsky's *Pictures at an Exhibition* displays an overwhelming command of orchestral tone-colour. Even where there is a certain romantic pathos in the piano original, as in *The Great Gate of Kiev*, Ravel's version finds sharp contrasts of colour which in no way recall Strauss or Debussy.

Ravel's two operas, *L'Heure espagnole* (1907) and *L'Enfant et les sortilèges* (1920), are so removed from the Wagnerian and Straussian

2 Emancipation

Art that seeks to express emotion is in principle hostile to form. Traditional models constrict the artist, like a garment that has not been made for him. However, in romantic and post-romantic music traditional forms remained intact in many respects. Certain schemes of construction were preserved as though they were laws of nature. The conventions of musical expression that were the crystallisation of centuries of standardised practice seemed fixed and immutable. Rhythm and metre were felt to be identical; the bar divided into two, three or four units with an accent on the first beat was the norm. Period or phrase structure followed an equally rigid rule: four-, eight- and sixteen-bar complexes were standard. The fixed sequence of triads in the tonal cadence governed endings and other elements of musical form. Melody and harmony existed in a state of mutual dependence from which they could break away only for short passages.

The presentation of musical ideas was as thoroughly bound by these rules of construction as the words of a lyric poem are by rhythm or metre. The situation was taken for granted in elementary and higher musical education. So far as the European conservatoires were concerned, classical rules of metre and period-form and the rules of tonality were sacrosanct. Although the works of the great classical masters were held up as objects of admiration and were recommended for study and imitation, they embodied techniques quite different from those which teachers recommended. Mozart, for example, uses a strikingly large number of melodic ideas or 'themes' which run right against periodic rules. Groups of five, seven or nine bars also frequently occur in Haydn and are of great formal significance. Classical composers frequently ignored laws of metre by using rhythms that could not be measured in terms of simple two-, three- and four-unit patterns. And the Viennese masters were only too pleased to make light of tonality and its symbol, the cadence. In the slow introduction to the first movement of Mozart's C major string quartet K.465, the underlying tonality is cunningly and skilfully concealed, though the syncopated entry of the second voice also plays a role by disguising the metre. The tonality of the finale of the G minor Symphony K.550 is a similar instance, not to mention the final banquet scene of *Don Giovanni*. All these features were redoubled in Beethoven. Much as his symphonies and chamber music seemed to enshrine traditional rules of metre, his rhythms broke through confines of this kind. The finale of the Ninth Symphony, with its blend of pot-pourri, variations and double fugue, was such an irreverent assault on traditional form that the theoreticians were left bewildered.

In many periods of European music there has been a clear distinction between poetry and prose, that is, between rigorously ordered metres and free melodic writing. The distinction is found in a concrete form with the operatic aria and the recitative. Yet during the eighteenth century a verse- or rhyme-like organisation of musical language became standard. Even in a musico-dramatic style as closely bound to word-rhythms as Wagner's, musical ideas are organised primarily according to verse- or rhyme-like patterns. The same is true of Brahms, though he was particularly ready to override rigid metric and periodic rules. The overall classical and romantic tradition was so strong, however, that deviations from the rules were regarded as mere irregularities, or even as 'infringements': that is, as violations of the due process of composition. It mattered little that such infringements became more and more frequent.

It was only when the flood-tide of chromaticism brought music to the brink of tonality and beyond, that these taboos of form and organisation were overcome. The chronology of the process is hard to establish. First steps towards a 'musical prose' are to be found in Mussorgsky, more so in his vocal than in his instrumental works. In Germany too, Reger showed all the signs of growing emancipation. The concept of a 'musical prose' embraces all attempts to release the different elements of music from the constraints of symmetrical organisation. In Reger's case this is true not only of complicated large-scale forms, but also of straightforward compositions such as the sixty songs he called *Schlichte Weisen* ('Simple Tunes'). Four-, eight- and sixteen-bar patterns are almost wholly absent in these songs, and the melodies for the most part avoid the degrees of the

(*below*) Introduction to Mozart's 'Dissonance' Quartet, K.465, showing 'false' contradictions of metre.
(*right*) The song 'Du lehnest wider eine silberweide' from Schoenberg's *Buch der hängenden Gärten.* Unresolved dissonances at the end of lines and phrases are shown in red.

scale. Alban Berg, in his essay of 1924 'Why is Schoenberg's music so difficult to understand?', recalls that Reger himself spoke of his style as a kind of musical prose. The same development appears relatively early in Schoenberg. His melodic writing assumes a clear prose-like character in proportion as it frees itself from Wagnerian models: his melodies dispense with symmetrical periodic forms and adopt new, less rigid proportions. Berg sees this as the main reason why Schoenberg's music is so difficult to understand.

However, this is certainly not the only reason. From about 1906 onwards the difference between consonance and dissonance in Schoenberg's music becomes increasingly blurred. Chords which had formerly been used only as passing harmonies, and had been carefully prepared, are now allowed to stand alone and are even used to round off sections or movements. Once it no longer seemed obligatory to resolve a dissonance into a triad, all combinations of notes became, in principle, equal. Schoenberg's First Chamber Symphony in E major was written in 1906. It contains chords of as many as six notes, arranged in fourths. Long passages are dominated

die Wei- den seh' ich, die sich   tie- fer hei- gen   und Blu- men, die ver-

- streut im Was- ser fah- ren

by the whole-tone scale and harmony based on it. In the second String Quartet in F sharp minor (written between 1907 and 1908), Schoenberg goes a step further. The last two movements, where a solo soprano joins the four stringed instruments, dispense with key signatures, which until this time had been customary. Furthermore, the music is not centred around a tonic and thus is not in any tonality. In the opening words of Stefan George's text: 'Ich fühle luft von anderem planeten' ('I breathe the air of another planet'). Shortly afterwards came the Two Songs Op. 14 and the fifteen poems from *Das Buch der hängenden Gärten* also by George. The thirteenth of these songs, 'Du lehnest wider eine silberweide' ('You lean against a silver willow'), sketched and completed on 27 September 1908, is the first composition by Schoenberg that is not in any key. In the other songs in the cycle too, the centuries-old principle of tonality is suspended. The music of Europe had entered a new epoch.

This 'style of freedom' did not stop with the suspension of tonal ties and the emancipation of the dissonance. Schoenberg produced in quick succession a large number of very varied works, all of which are alive with the excitement of discoveries such as European music had not known since 1600. The new style appears in the Three Piano Pieces Op. 11, the Five Orchestral Pieces Op. 16, and the mono-drama *Erwartung* Op. 17. The latter, a psycho-dramatical stage work, marks the disappearance of the remnants of symphonic and thematic working that had still governed some of the George Lieder and extensive passages in the Orchestral Pieces. In *Erwartung* the concept of a 'musical prose' has been 'thought through' to the end. Pure-musical relationships are restricted to chords and motifs. The music is subjected to a process of permanent variation. Towering ten- and eleven-note chords dispel any remaining traces of traditional consonance. One eleven-part chord in *Erwartung* uses every note of the chromatic scale with the exception of G sharp. Because Schoenberg completely dispenses with the repetition of musical ideas, dimensions become highly curtailed. The Three Pieces for Chamber Orchestra, the third of which remained a fragment, are extremely short miniatures dating from as early as February 1910. They provide the stepping-stone to the micro-forms which Webern favoured between 1910 and 1924. Schoenberg himself made further use of these radically abbreviated forms in the Six Little Piano Pieces (1911) and in some of the melodramas of *Pierrot Lunaire* (1912), before giving them up.

During the same period modern music outside Germany was moving towards a revolution in the field of rhythm. The Russian innovators of 1860 had already felt hampered by the classical two- or three-beat bar and had done something to break away from it. Later, Bartók and Stravinsky began to use syncopated displace-ments of accent which upset the equilibrium of the bar. Bartók's folk-song researches in Hungary, Rumania and Bulgaria in 1905 had shown him rhythms which diverged from the symmetrical norms of Central European music. He found 'prime-number' metres, such as 7/8, 5/8, 11/8 and so on, and asymmetrical accents within traditional metres. Thus, an 8/8 bar might be composed of 3+3+2 or 3+2+3 or 2+3+3 crotchets and would create a

totally different effect from a classical 4/4 bar of the same length.
Besides these new metrical schemes, the researches also unearthed
polymetric combinations which were the complete antithesis of the
simple, traditional sense of rhythm. Bartók was addicted to these
metres and rhythms throughout his creative life. They dominate the
style of his early piano works, including the collection *For Children*,
and the later Fifth String Quartet (1934), the Music for strings,
percussion and celesta (1936) and the six Bulgarian Dances from
Mikrokosmos.

This use of metres and rhythms that differ from the older two-
and three-unit types is also symptomatic of the new prose style of
musical thinking. It corresponds to the freeing of phrase or period
structure from classical rules. Rhythm and form are thus brought
into a new kind of relationship – one which was developed methodically after 1940. In Bartók's case, the dance and folk-song origins
of the new rhythms are always clearly recognisable, although
he himself, apart from a few early works, never merely imitated
folk-music.

Stravinsky in his youth was as much stirred by Russian folk-
music as Bartók was by the folk-music of the Balkans. The results
are most strikingly shown in the great ballet scores he wrote for
Diaghilev in 1911 and 1912. *Petrushka* contains perpetually varying
time-signatures, and different time-signatures used simultaneously.
In the next ballet, *Le Sacre du printemps*, he takes the principle to
the limit. In the last section in particular, the 'Danse sacrale', the
metre ranges constantly between 2/16 and 5/16. Asymmetry has
become the norm. *Le Sacre* marks the climax in the break-up of

Diaghilev's dancers found their own solution (*below*) to the problem of keeping time while working on the finale to Ravel's *Daphnis et Chloé*. (*right*) The impresario himself, drawn by Christopher Wood, watches from the wings. Worse was in store for Diaghilev's company when Stravinsky gave him the score of *Le Sacre du printemps*, which was at first said to be undanceable.

Ser - ge Dia - ghi - lev! Ser - ge Dia - ghi - lev! Ser - ge Dia - ghi - lev!

traditional metres. The rehearsals with Diaghilev's company showed what demands the new rhythms made on the dancers. Ravel's harmless 5/4 rhythms in *Daphnis et Chloé* had been difficult enough, but they were far surpassed by Stravinsky's. Before, the dancers had used the device of chanting the name 'Ser-ge Dia-ghi-lev' in chorus; this time there could be no short cuts. The dancer and choreographer Serge Lifar later vehemently condemned *Le Sacre* because he claimed the music could not be danced. The work's first performance in the Théâtre des Champs-Élysées in Paris on 29 May 1913 ended in one of the greatest public uproars of the century. Its blend of dissonant polytonality and new rhythms was more than the premiere audience could endure.

In point of fact, the new music of composers such as Bartók and Stravinsky made for an enrichment of rhythm. Western music had become increasingly impoverished in rhythm and metre since the high point of polyphony in the sixteenth century. We can see an enormous difference if we compare our music with the musical heritages of non-European cultures, particularly of India and central Africa. However, a hidden law of equilibrium seems to apply to the different elements of which music is made up. A bias towards polyphony, towards independent, simultaneously-sounding melodic parts, brings with it an automatic decline in the field of rhythm. Harmony can play differing roles here. If it evolves according to the rules of the tonal cadence, whereby given chord-progressions are standardised, the development of rhythm is shackled. On the other hand, if chords are used primarily for their sound-value – non-functionally, in other words – they can be used to give strong

(*below*) Stravinsky:
Le Sacre du printemps,
'Danse Sacrale'.

(*right*) The Indian 'sam' is delayed
until the very last beat of this
excerpt from an extended piece.

emphasis to the rhythmic accents. In Stravinsky and Bartók harmony plays this second role. In consequence it must break with the
rules of the cadence.

The move towards greater freedom in the years preceding the
First World War was not limited to tonality and rhythm. Both of
these had been cases of dispensing with stable points of equilibrium.
The role of the tonic within tonality, e.g. of the note C in a piece in
the key of C, corresponds to the stable, regularly-recurring accent
in the field of rhythm, the down-beat in the European bar, which is
oddly analogous to the *sam* in the quantitative metres of Indian
music.

But the process of revision did not stop here. The actual system of
notes no longer seemed adequate. Note-systems in the music of all
civilisations are founded on natural sound-phenomena. Ever since
the Greek acoustical theorists, or since the researches of the Chinese
for that matter, the first intervals of the overtone series (octave, fifth
and fourth) had provided the accepted fixed points of systems of
music. Scales were constructed by adding fifths, or fifths and
descending fourths. Four intervals of this kind produce the pentatonic scale, the five-note scale composed of whole tones and minor

thirds that has been preserved in Scottish and Irish folk-music and still survives in the music of China. By adding two more fifths to the pentatonic scale, we get the seven-note scales that were used in Greek music and the church modes, as well as in classical Indian music. Finally, if we complete the circle of fifths, we obtain the semitones that lie between the diatonic steps of the seven-note scale. Increasingly these 'natural' intervals were found to be impure, so that adjustments became necessary. This adjusted twelve-note scale is the foundation of our Western note-system, and is also the foundation of Chinese and Indian practice. Naturally, both classical tonal Western music and Eastern music are founded on selections made from the total sum of possibilities.

However, once the use of an 'unnatural', mathematical division of the octave had been accepted, it became theoretically possible to go a step further. Intervals smaller than a semitone had occurred in the music of many nations for thousands of years. We know that ancient Greek music employed 'chroai', micro-intervals within the tetrachord. The theoretician Aristoxenos even discussed quarter-, three-quarter- and three eighth-tones. Possibly this was only an explanation in theory of something oriental music had long prac-

Pentatonic scale:

a
'S ole an ob-air do theach-dair-ean cad-al, Hù rù ag-us hiul-lir-in o—ho ro Bean

òg a' chùil chleach-daich aig bail-e 'ga càr—adh, Ho ro hù aig tois-each na tràghad

b

c Moderato

tised. Indian music, for example, uses so-called *srutis*, or intervals smaller than a semitone.

In the twentieth century mounting pressure on the necessarily restricted scope of the semitonal scale led to new theories and experiments, principally those in bichromaticism. Mathematical bisection of the semitone had already been shown to be practicable by the end of the nineteenth century. G. A. Behrens-Senegalden patented a quarter-tone piano in 1892. But it was not until 1924 that the Czech firm of August Foerster actually constructed a quarter-tone grand piano of its own design.

Three examples of pentatonicism in folk-music:
(a) A Gaelic work-song from the Isle of Barra;
(b) The Irish air 'What is that to him?';
(c) A Chinese wedding-march.

One of the first composers to use the quarter-tone system was Richard H. Stein, born in Halle in 1882. Having written a doctoral dissertation on the psychological foundations of Wundt's ethics, he undertook scientific research into the expansion of the note-system. In 1909, 'on the birthday of Richard Wagner' as he wrote at the end of his pamphlet, he completed an outline of his quarter-tone system, though he had already published two quarter-tone *Concert Pieces* for cello and piano in 1906. Later he repudiated his ideas and these works. He did not wish to be identified with a quarter-tone school which started from quite different and, as he thought, erroneous assumptions.

In Russia, some quarter-tone experiments had also been made towards the end of the nineteenth century. The composer Ivan Vyshnegradsky, born in St Petersburg in 1893 but resident in Paris from 1922, took up these threads and devoted all his energies to exploring the concept of bichromaticism. After making his own two-manual quarter-tone piano, he published an introduction to the theory of quarter-tone harmony in Paris in 1933. His compositions include orchestral works, such as *Dithyramb* and *Prelude and Fugue*, a string quartet, and pieces for solo violin, quarter-tone clarinet and quarter-tone piano.

Busoni outlined a possible expansion of the semitonal system in his *Sketch of a new aesthetic of music* (1906). However, he did not advocate the principle of bichromaticism. He suggested a division of the whole tone into three, whereby the octave C–C would be composed of eighteen third-tone steps. A chromatic shift into the octave C sharp–C sharp would necessarily produce a second eighteen-note scale. Together the two scales would form a thirty-six-note, sixth-tone, system. Busoni himself did not compose in this system, but he continued to defend it into the 1920s.

In Berlin at this time was the Czech composer Alois Hába (born 1893). He had studied composition at the Prague Conservatoire under Vítěslav Novak from 1914–15, and had then become a pupil of Franz Schreker in Vienna, whom he followed to the Berliner Hochschule für Musik in 1921. In 1919 Hába composed his first

A passage from Hába's *String Quartet No. 1.*

string quartet in the quarter-tone system and the work was first performed on 31 July 1921 at the opening concert of the Donaueschingen Music Festival. Since then he has not only produced a large number of quarter-tone works but has encouraged the construction of quarter-tone instruments, including the Foerster piano mentioned earlier and a quarter-tone clarinet. In 1923 Hába founded a class in quarter-tone composition at the Prague Conservatoire, which has attracted numerous students from many countries. Other musical academies have since followed suit, such as the conservatoire in Cairo.

In his theoretical writings Hába has offered an evolutionary explanation of quarter-tones. He sees them as one stage on the road from simplicity to complexity. In his essay on note-differences and the scope of musical styles he writes:

We can assume that man's greatest desire, to bring natural phenomena under the most wide-ranging conscious control, will also induce musicians to bring under conscious control all the frequencies that the ear can distinguish.

Busoni (1866–1924), one of the greatest pianists of his time, initiated a new pianistic style with his transcriptions of Liszt and Bach, particularly the *Fantasia Contrappuntistica* on Bach's outlines. His Second Sonatina comes near to Schoenbergian atonality. Most of Busoni's life was spent in Germany, where he wrote or had performed his four operas.

This shows that Hába did not want to stop at quarter-tones. Indeed, stimulated by Busoni, he also composed in sixth-tones, in the Fifth String Quartet (1923) and a Duo for two violins (1927). In fact, he has gone further still and used twelfth-tones, in other words an octave containing seventy-two steps. With his extraordinarily acute ear he can distinguish these micro-intervals, which only few instruments can play.

Hába later backed up his theory and his system with research into Moravian folk-music. He found, as Bartók and Kodály had done in the Balkans, that there are divergences from the intervals of the seven-note scale in folk-song which are not to be dismissed as mere bad intonation. These are notes which differ from tempered whole tones and semitones by a quarter, a sixth, a third or an eighth of a tone. The results are interesting because they show once more, as so often in the history of the arts, how the works of art of an advanced period of intellectual development can have affinities with archaic and apparently primitive practices. We touch on similar questions when we compare the tempered chromatic scale with the intervals of the overtone series. From the seventh overtone on, and more so from the eleventh, we find intervals which lie outside our standard semitonal universe. A mathematical process of division helps the ear to distinguish these 'natural' intervals.

In Hába's quarter-tone opera *Mother* (first performed on 17 May 1931 in Munich) bichromaticism was at first linked to non-tonal music in the Schoenbergian sense. Other advocates of quarter-tones such as Stein started from tonal assumptions. In his later works Hába has written tonal music in which quarter- or sixth-tones are used merely as variants. Here the whole process of bichromaticism has returned to its ancient roots, thereby providing a bridge back to the note-systems of non-European civilisations such as those of India and Arabia. Indeed, the so-called 'enharmonic' tetrachord of the Greek theorists consists of a quarter-tone division of the bottom interval of the tetrachord. The *srutis* of Indian music are also close to our mathematical quarter-tones, as they divide the octave into twenty-two steps.

A Hungarian lament of the type
collected by Kodály and Bartók.
The arrows indicate micro-tonal sharpenings
and flattenings in pitch.

It is a point of controversy whether micro-tones, or better, micro-intervals, are musically necessary. Schoenberg discusses the issue in his *Harmonielehre*. He speaks of a 'compromise between the natural intervals and our inability to use them'. He believes that our note-system will merge into a higher scheme as did the church modes. Besides third-, quarter-, sixth- and eighth-tones he mentions an octave of fifty-three equal parts which has the advantage of containing the purest consonance-relations. But for Schoenberg polyphony is more important than a multiplication of degrees. He also rejects on principle all exotic, non-European influences on Western music, which latter he sees as the most complete yet to have evolved.

A system of composition can equally well be founded on micro-intervals as on semitones. It is clear that a twenty-four-note series can be manipulated in just the same way as a twelve-note one. But as listeners still find enough difficulties in dealing with twelve-note music, such a development would appear premature. The ear can of course be trained, and the faculties of the brain developed, so that if one day it becomes as easy to take in twelve-note constructions as is now possible with tonal cadences, then the question of micro-tone composition can once more be raised. But until then composers will have to be content to use quarter-tones and smaller intervals merely as occasional enrichments of melodic and harmonic ideas, not as means of construction. This is the light in which we should see the later quarter- and sixth-tone compositions of Alois Hába. Indeed, he was able with them to come to terms with the Communist aesthetic regulations in force in Czechoslovakia after 1948.

A large number of other composers and musicologists have also worked with bichromaticism. For example, Willi von Moellendorf has been an advocate of quarter-tone music since 1917, both as theoretician and composer. He has also invented a harmonium with a new quarter-tone keyboard. The Mexican composer Julian Carrillo (born 1875) has been the greatest pioneer of micro-tonal music in the New World. He uses a strict mathematical method of note-division, and employs intervals of quarter-, eighth- and sixteenth-tones. In 1926 the League of Composers in New York performed works of Carrillo containing such intervals. A harp-zither of his own invention has strings for ninety-six subdivisions within the octave, and he also uses a harp which has a mere sixty-four. His *Concertino*, which calls for these instruments, was performed by Stokowski and the Philadelphia Orchestra in 1927.

Composers who have occasionally incorporated quarter-tones into otherwise chromatic compositions include Ernest Bloch in his Piano Quintet, Georges Enesco in his opera *Oedipus*, and Bartók in his Sonata for Solo Violin. The violinist Rudolf Kolisch, a friend of Bartók, has said that the quarter- and two-thirds-tones in this latter work contribute to the thematic substance and are not used merely for colour.

The universe of musical sounds is a continuum. All scales, however many notes they contain, are, as we have already seen, only selections from the sum of possibilities. The organic development of the ear and of musical theory, as much as mere chance, lies behind these selections. The technical scope of different instruments and the styles of singing of different cultures have affected the evolution of scales and note-systems from ancient times. If we were to collect all known natural and tempered intervals into one scale, we should get a note-system with hundreds of steps within the octave. But by doing so we should virtually have returned to the continuum, as far as performance and listening are concerned.

Music that uses micro-intervals of a quarter-tone or less cannot be notated in normal fashion. There has been no lack of attempts to extend notation. Hába's quarter-tone notation is modelled on traditional semitone notation, and can be adjusted – with some difficulty

3 Noise and timbre

Until the present day, composers drew on a very small part of the entire world of sounds. Even in the case of musical sounds proper (*Töne*) we saw that only a few of the infinite number of infinitely small gradations within the continuum have ever been used to form systems of notes. But musical sounds are themselves only one small element in the unlimited number of possible acoustical phenomena. The everyday world is filled with acoustical events, both natural and man-made. They surround us as an aura of virtually uninterrupted auditory perceptions. We are so accustomed to most of them that they impinge on our consciousness only by standing out in some way from the common run of perceptual experiences. The songs of the birds are with us all the year round, ranging from the unattractive single-note cries of sparrows and crows to the highly melodic songs of blackbirds and nightingales. Rain, thunder and hail form a frequently recurring background to our daily life. The rush of river-waters and the roar of the sea are characteristic of the way in which we experience natural phenomena. Men at all times have used music in order to mirror this vast scheme of sounds and noises, not so much by creating a replica of acoustical phenomena as by endowing this highly varied raw material with artistic form.

In all advanced civilisations musical sounds rank higher than noises (*Geräusche*) in the hierarchy of musical values. By 'musical sound' (*Ton*) we mean a simple acoustical event definable in terms of a given number of vibrations per second. A pure sine-wave sound or 'sinus-tone' cannot, however, be produced on traditional instruments, although the sound of a tuning-fork or a note blown on a recorder comes close to it. In practical music-making we use mostly 'composite sounds' (*Klänge*), or, in physical terms, musical sounds each of which is supplemented by a pyramid of simultaneously-sounding overtones. A composite sound containing several different pyramids of overtones is called a note-mixture. These occur in church bells, the sound of struck metal plates or pipes, and the like.

With all these acoustical phenomena the ear can clearly distinguish one or more definite pitches, but there are other, more complex phenomena in which a predominant frequency can no longer be discerned. These are noises (*Geräusche*), which form the major part of what our ears perceive. Physics has various definitions of the word 'noise', all slightly different. We shall define it as an acoustical event in which a large number of frequencies and their associated pyramids of overtones are present simultaneously. Within the totality of noises there is an infinite number of such frequency-structures. The fewer the frequencies within a given frequency-range, the more closely such noises approach musical sounds of definite pitch; sounds consisting of a very large number of frequencies are what we normally know as 'noises'. The latter are analogous in structure to white light, in which all the other colours of the spectrum are blended.

Instruments producing noises have long since had a place in classical Western music. Even the timbres of stringed and wind instruments (in physical terms, chordophones and aerophones) have their accretions of noises and are given individual definition by noises. Percussion instruments – drums, rattles or shaken idiophones, metal idiophones and the rest – produce a sound of a predominantly noise-like character, though even here the frontiers are not precisely marked: there are drums, such as timpani, which produce notes of definite pitch. Yet all these percussion instruments furnish only a small selection from the boundless world of possible noises, and in Western music they have played only a minor role, far less important than that of sounds of definite pitch.

It cannot be contested that noises have their place in music. Mozart and Beethoven occasionally used the percussion effects of 'Turkish' or janissary music, which were scarcely known in western Europe at the time. The music is a source of exotic colour in *Die Entführung* and expresses animated joy in the short B flat march in the finale of the Ninth Symphony. Three instruments make up the sound: a bass drum, cymbals and triangle. With the growing interest of the romantics in the music of different civilisations, non-European percussion instruments began to come into Western music. But traditional music teaching regarded them as intruders; even as dedicated a supporter of the modern movement as Hermann

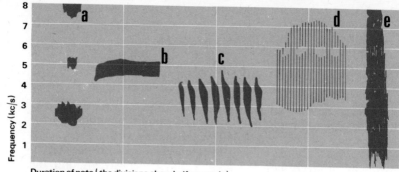

Duration of note (the divisions show half-seconds)

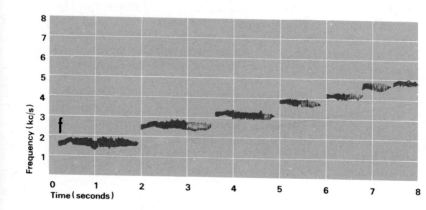

Scherchen described percussion instruments as 'unpitched and anti-musical'. A reaction against such a restricted musical palette was not long in coming. On 11 March 1913 the Italian futurist Luigi Russolo wrote a letter to his friend and colleague Balilla Pratella in which he sketched out a new music of noise. He was influenced by the experimental poetry of Marinetti, who had written a war poem in which the sounds of weapons were depicted by syllables, vowels and consonants. Russolo called for a methodical investigation of noises and suggested a list distinguishing six types:

1 Bangs, thunderclaps, explosions, etc.
2 Whistles, hisses, snorts.
3 Whispers, murmurs, rustling, gurgling.

The distinction between musical sounds, composite sounds and noises can be perceived quite clearly in the songs of different birds. A three-diagram series of bird notes, scaled by frequency and time, illustrates these tonal qualities. (a) nightingale, very pure, with harmonics; (b) white-throated sparrow, clear whistle; (c) marsh warbler, musical trill; (d) clay-coloured sparrow, a toneless buzz; (e) budgerigar, a noisy flight squawk. The song of the pileated tinamou (f) is the purest, sounding like a flute with no overtones at all – i.e. pure *Ton*. By contrast, the corn bunting's song (g) has a large range of frequencies and a very short duration. Perceived as a series of clicks, it may be classed as noise (*Geräusch*).

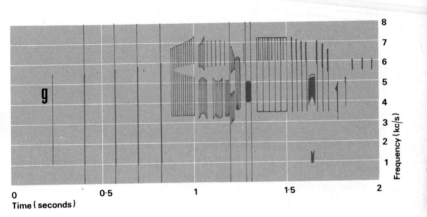

4 Screams, shrieks, buzzing, crackling, sounds produced by friction.
5 Sounds produced by striking metal, wood, stone, china, etc.
6 Animal and human cries – roars, howls, laughter, sobs, sighs, etc.

Sounds of this kind had always been used for background effects in the theatre, but in music they were a novelty. In an enthusiastic manifesto of 1912 Pratella had himself appealed for the songs of factories, warships, motor-cars and aeroplanes; he exhorted musicians to take due account of the empire of the machine and the all-conquering power of electricity.

The self-explanatory name of this new art of noise was *bruitismo*. The futurists' inventory of instruments was at once primitive and ominous. They planned to use machine guns, sirens and steam-whistles. Russolo later built a *rumor-armonio* which could produce micro-intervals in addition to countless noises.

Only a little of the music of the futurists has survived, some of it on gramophone records. The compositions of Pratella and Russolo are of very limited artistic value. They consist mostly of simple melodic ideas with an accompanying palette of noises. But the notion of building musical forms from noises survived. It re-appeared in Stravinsky's *L'Histoire du soldat* (1918), where in the final March of the Devil the voices of the melodic instruments die away and the last word is left to the drums. Stravinsky's score calls for two side drums of different sizes without snares, one side drum with snares, a small drum with snares, a bass drum, cymbals, tambourine and triangle, all played by one percussionist.

Like noise, timbre has been regarded as a 'non-essential' in traditional European orchestral music, as a kind of ornamental trimming. It is common practice in a classical score for a melody to be switched from one instrument to another without alteration to the musical substance. This relative indifference to colour is a relic of the *ad libitum* instrumentation of the Middle Ages. Only since the eighteenth century has timbre assumed an important role in composition. The ever-increasing differentiation of instrumental timbres in romantic and impressionist music meant that colour eventually gained an independent significance.

Schoenberg was one of the first musical theoreticians to discuss the properties of musical sound. In the *Harmonielehre* of 1911 he distinguishes three properties: pitch, colour, and intensity. He makes the point that until then only pitch had been measured, and that little attempt had been made to measure or in any way organise colour or intensity. In the half-century since he wrote, a considerable quantity of literature on dynamics and timbre has been produced but we have still no really systematic understanding of either subject. Schoenberg pursues the topic further and finally defines pitch as one of the dimensions of timbre ('tone-colour'): 'Pitch is in fact simply tone-colour, measured in one direction.' . . . He proceeds to

imagine a future time when music would be constructed from 'timbre-melodies' (*Klangfarbenmelodien*). Such music could give expression to our dreams, he says; it would speak to men of fine sensibilities and developed minds who could take pleasure in such subtle things. Schoenberg gives a rough outline of his plan in this final chapter of the *Harmonielehre*. He argues that since melodic shapes can be created from varying pitches, successions of different timbres ought also to produce analogous shapes of their own. Like pitch-structures, timbre-structures should have an analysable internal organisation. The relations of one timbre to another should be dictated by a logic comparable to that underlying changes in pitch.

In fact, Schoenberg had already experimented with timbre in the third of the Five Pieces for Orchestra Op. 16, which he completed in Steinkirchen on 1 July 1909. At the request of his publisher Schoenberg gave the piece a title: 'Summer morning by a lake', adding the word 'Colours' in brackets. The special technique he uses here consists of presenting successions of chords, each with various combinations of timbres. The five-part chord:

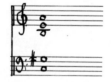

is played first by two flutes, clarinet, bassoon and solo viola. The four upper instruments are soon replaced by cor anglais, second bassoon, horn and trumpet, with the viola still supplying the lowest note. A C on the solo double bass provides a rhythmic ornamentation, imitating the viola in hocket style. This treatment of the first chord lasts for three bars. Other chords then follow in successive bars. From the seventh bar further solo melodic ideas emerge, on the bass clarinet, clarinet, bassoon, trombone and three muted double basses. Schoenberg observes in a footnote: 'The chords must change so gently that no emphasis can be perceived at the instrumental entries, and so that the change is made apparent only through the new colour.' Not content with this, Schoenberg provides a note for performance, which is printed in the score:

In this piece the conductor's task is not to bring out those individual voices which seem to him thematically important, nor to even out supposedly unbalanced mixtures of sounds. Where one part is to stand out more than the others, it is scored to that effect and the sounds are not to be evened out. The conductor's task is to ensure that each instrument plays at the exact dynamic level indicated: subjectively exact in terms of the instrument itself and not objectively in relation to the overall sound.

Schoenberg showed the score to Mahler, who said he could not read it. Richard Strauss declined his invitation to conduct the first performance. The music had entered new worlds where even the best musical minds of 1909 could not find their bearings.

The Five Pieces were first performed in London on 3 September 1912, under Henry Wood. Most critics reacted unfavourably. *The Times* described the work as 'an essay in dissonance', and said it was as incomprehensible as a Tibetan poem. Hugo Leichtentritt, the Berlin musicologist and critic, wrote:

What frightening visions these sounds arouse! What ghastly nightmares they evoke! And, alas, nothing in the way of joy or light, nothing of what makes life worth living! How poor our descendants will be if they take this joyless, careworn Schoenberg as their epitome of the sensibility of our age!

There was thus a complete failure to understand the artistic intention of the pieces, the third in particular. This is a familiar enough situation in the history of the arts. The artist's contemporaries either completely fail to see what he is aiming at in his works and what is new in them, or they see only negative qualities which are not relevant and which when emphasised lead to distortion and caricature.

Long before Schoenberg's notion of the *Klangfarbenmelodie* was taken up by young composers in about 1950, it was extended by some of his pupils. Webern's Five Pieces for Orchestra Op. 10 were written between 1911 and 1913. They constitute a kind of sublimated creative reaction to Schoenberg's Opus 16. Like Schoenberg's Pieces, the five movements, which carry only tempo markings in the

'Rückkehr': Webern's third Orchestral Piece, Op. 10, analysed by instrumental groupings to show how a music of *Klangfarben* may be organised from distinct instrumental timbres.

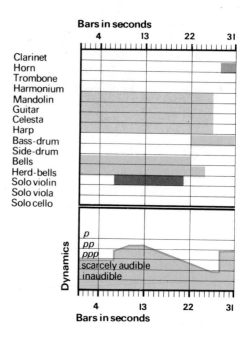

score, were given titles indicative of moods for their premiere in Vienna: *Urbild* ('Archetype'), *Verwandlung* ('Transformation'), *Rückkehr* ('Return'), *Erinnerung* ('Remembrance'), and *Seele* ('Spirit'). All parts in the work are written for solo players, and the instrumentation has a chamber-music character like that of Schoenberg's Chamber Symphony for fifteen instruments of 1906. The strings consist of one violin, one viola, one cello and one double bass. Woodwind is represented by flute (and piccolo), oboe, B flat clarinet (and bass clarinet) and E flat clarinet; brass by horn, trumpet and trombone. In addition there are a harmonium, celesta, mandolin, guitar and harp, and eight percussion instruments including glockenspiel, xylophone, herd bells and large bells.

The score shows no traces of thematic working, and even motivic

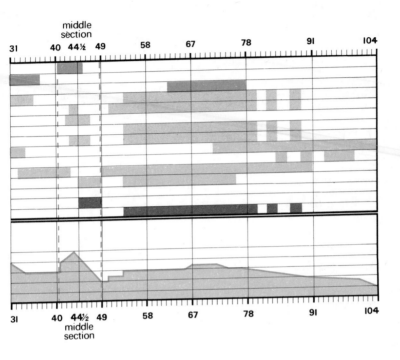

middle
section

31   40 44½ 49   58   67   78   91   104

relationships are rare. On few occasions do notes sound together as chords. The rhythms are fully asymmetrical. The whole work is extraordinarily rich in dynamic subtleties, particularly in gradations of *pianissimo*. The second piece lasts only fourteen seconds; the longest, the third, lasts one minute forty-five seconds. In a world of such highly compressed forms, individual timbres stand out all the more clearly. They generate textures which are quite different from those of traditional orchestral music. Webern manipulates them so convincingly that we can, indeed must, speak of a music of *Klangfarben*. The way in which he organises colour is quite different in detail from Schoenberg's third Piece for Orchestra. Webern does not merely provide the chords with shifting instrumental colours. For example, in the relatively longer third piece, *Rückkehr*, timbre

A simple invention form is the basis for
the fourth scene of Act 3 of *Wozzeck*, with
a six-part chord used on various steps of the
scale for varying musico-dramatic effects.
(*right*) The same scene in the London
production of Berg's opera.

itself creates the form. Its opening is a flurry of colour, with a tremolo chord D-E-A on guitar and mandolin, a trill on the note E by bells and herd bells, a B flat on the celesta, and the effect special to the harp produced by playing one note on two strings alternately (in this case two notes, G sharp and C sharp). To these are added the solo violin and later the horn, playing tiny melodic fragments whose intervals are properties of the colour, in the sense laid down by Schoenberg. The middle section of the piece occupies only two bars and contains new timbres such as clarinet, muted cello and muted viola. There follows a varied reprise of the opening, which introduces the new timbres of the harmonium and muted trombone. Similar procedures govern the sonorities of the other four pieces. With the utmost sensitivity and imagination Webern explores the new world of musical ideas opened up by Schoenberg's Opus 16. His spare, chamber-like orchestral works always stayed in this world. Although the strict laws of technical construction came later, his dodecaphonic works after 1924 continued to be illuminated by the shifting spectra of timbres of Opus 10 and subsequent works.

Alban Berg uses timbre as a means of construction in no less artistic a fashion. But Berg is far more disposed to communicate than Webern. If he uses new techniques, he gives them clear prominence. Further, he is willing to justify them on, as it were, illustrative grounds. Many details in the score of *Wozzeck* (composed between 1914 and 1921) illustrate the use of orchestral colour as a means of construction. In one scene this almost amounts to an explicit demonstration. This is the famous fourth scene of Act 3, which takes place by the pond at night and leads to the death of Wozzeck, who is looking for the knife with which he has stabbed Marie. For this scene Berg uses one of the invention forms which underlie the whole act. These forms consist of elementary musical ideas, such as a theme, a note or a rhythm, which are used in wholly novel structural ways. The fourth scene is based on a six-part chord consisting of a fixed pattern of intervals: minor third, minor third, major third, fifth and whole tone. In the course of the scene the chord is constantly transposed on to new steps of the scale. It returns to its

Berg (1885–1936) and Webern (1883–1945), near Vienna
in 1912. Where the one sought to justify his new ideas
within a traditional framework, the other created
a new framework to be its own justification. They were
Schoenberg's two most celebrated and influential
pupils and remained lifelong friends.

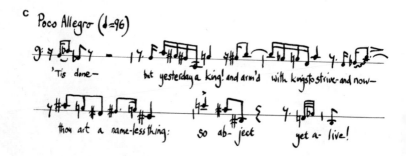

original position only at the end of the scene, in the form B flat-C sharp-E-G sharp-E flat-F. Berg first paints the chord in the strong variegated colours of the wind, with *forte* flutes, oboes, clarinets, bass clarinet, bassoons and horns. This merges into a *pianissimo* chord on a few instruments only, which is soon taken up, *pppp*, by muted violins and violas. At the words: 'So! Da hinunter!' the chord is heard an octave lower, *fortissimo*, on violas, cellos and double basses. After Wozzeck's death, as the Captain and the Doctor are walking past the pond, it is heard again, this time held for eighteen bars on muted strings. The whole scene is rich in other instances of the illustrative use of orchestral timbre, to which Wozzeck's voice also contributes. As always in Berg, radical new methods are, so to speak, legitimised by being furnished with a

Sprechstimme notation in
(a) Humperdinck's *Königskinder;*
(b) Schoenberg's *Pierrot Lunaire;*
(c) Schoenberg's *Ode to Napoleon.*

63

traditional framework. Such uses of colour, which the Schoenberg school erected into a principle are frequently to be found in Richard Strauss, and even in Liszt and Berlioz. Berg's music always proclaims its connection with tradition. Although Schoenberg and Webern were always conscious of their own links with the past, as their theoretical writings show, in their music this awareness always took second place to their passion for new discoveries.

Further extensions of musical sound-material took place in the vocal field. In opera it had long been common practice to use speech (*Sprechstimme*) in addition to singing. The special form known as the melodrama – the reciting of a spoken text to instrumental accompaniment – had also been used by classical and romantic composers. But in both *Singspiel* and melodrama the spoken word merely followed the requirements of the text, whether verse or prose. In the melodramas of Rousseau (*Pygmalion*, 1762) or Benda (*Ariadne*, 1775), in the spoken scenes in Mozart's *Zaide*, in *Fidelio* or *Der Freischütz*, text and music are only very loosely co-ordinated. The spoken word gets free range within a generous allocation of bars.

Towards the end of the nineteenth century attempts were made in Germany to tie down the *Sprechstimme* more precisely and to connect it with notated music, both rhythmically and in terms of so-called 'speech-melody'. This was the origin of the *Sprechstimme* notation in Humperdinck's melodrama *Königskinder* (1897), which Schoenberg later amplified.

The score of *Pierrot Lunaire* (1912) shows the manifold possibilities of using the spoken voice in a musical context. Schoenberg ensures that the recitation takes place in strict time by using traditional notation. He also uses crosses for note-heads to indicate the line of the 'speech-melody', and the performer has to take her directions from them. One factor aggravates the problem. The sounds of speech cannot be precisely defined in terms of frequencies, which makes them essentially different from instrumental sounds. The characteristics of individual voices are also relevant. Some voices have a fairly precise intonation, while others are acoustically closer to the noise (*Geräusch*) than to the musical sound (*Ton*).

Schoenberg's *Sprechstimme* notation was a strictly personal expression of his vision of the new melodrama form. The acoustical side of the problem was a closed book to him. Despite its pitch and rhythm indications, the notation only gives hints and is quite incapable of plotting the intonation of speech exactly, if that was ever its aim. Little wonder that great difficulties were experienced in actual performance. Schoenberg's conception of a style of delivery halfway between speech and strict adherence to musical notation is extremely hard to achieve. Performances of *Pierrot Lunaire* were later recorded and the pitches of the different *Sprechstimmen* compared. One version, by the actress and singer Erika Wagner, met with Schoenberg's approval; another, by Wilma Mönckeberg, was less accurate in his opinion, but was in fact closer to the indications in the score. This surely implies that the spoken voice as such cannot be notated in traditional musical fashion. Only a new phonetic notation could solve this problem.

The same applies to the notation of noises. If we restrict ourselves to traditional percussion instruments such as drums, cymbals and so on, an approximate notation is sufficient, e.g. 'high drum', 'middle drum' and 'low drum'. But if we want to indicate the quality of a particular noise, our existing means are useless. Timbre too, when associated with a musical sound of definite pitch, can be indicated only by naming the instrument that produces it. Between the well-established timbres of a flute, a viola and a trombone, or for that matter between flute and piccolo, violin and viola, or trumpet and trombone, there are ranges of timbre which traditional instruments cannot attain. Like physical colours, tone-colours form a continuum from which individual gradations are selected arbitrarily or at random. The same applies to the timbres of pitched musical sounds of measurable frequency and noises, as well as to the noise-like sounds of human speech.

All these notions had been in the air for some decades. The first composers who dreamed of revitalising the raw material of music worked on their own, with no intellectual contact with each other. Their scores, experimenting with timbre, noises or *Sprechstimme*, or combinations of the three, remained unknown and unperformed for many years. Someone who heard works of this kind performed could not immediately tell that they were experiments in a new auditory language. The only composers who claimed publicly to be providing music with a new language were the Italian bruitists, Russolo and Pratella. Yet they were creatively too weak to produce music that would last or continue to be performed. True, Schoenberg's and Webern's *Klangfarben* structures were deliberately designed as means of renewing musical language. But their contemporaries did not understand their aims; it merely seemed that other, traditional relationships had been sacrificed. So the advance into a world of new sounds and new forms or organisation remained unnoticed and without influence. *Pierrot Lunaire*, though, made a strong impact in 1912, favourable as well as unfavourable. Schoenberg's *Sprechstimme* technique remained a powerful force in his own and his pupils' works. His short drama *Die glückliche Hand* (completed 1913) uses a whole chorus of *Sprechstimmen*, together with a sung chorus. Here was a strong dramatic contrast between the sung and the spoken word, which was to bear fruit later, notably in the opera *Moses und Aron*.

Berg further extended Schoenberg's *Sprechstimme* technique in *Wozzeck*. The first scene of Act 3 begins with Marie's reading from the Bible, recited in the manner of *Pierrot Lunaire*. Throughout the scene, speech with notated rhythm and intonation alternates with singing proper. The scene closes with a fugue, the first entry of which is spoken by Marie, with the other three parts played by solo viola, solo violin and solo double bass, all muted. This is not the only melodrama-form in *Wozzeck* but it is certainly the most important. There are various other places where Wozzeck himself and his partners have to speak instead of sing. The second scene of Act 1, for example, when Wozzeck and Andres are cutting firewood in the open fields, begins with a dialogue in *Sprechstimme*.

This use of the voice has nothing to do with the sung recitatives of traditional opera. Nor does it correspond to the simple spoken dialogue of the *Singspiel*, as in *Die Entführung*, *Fidelio* or *Der*

Freischütz. It was rather that the tentative experiment Schoenberg made in *Pierrot Lunaire* gave rise to a new kind of musical drama, with the voice playing a part somewhat comparable to the sounds of the enlarged percussion section in the modern symphony orchestra. The new techniques proved to be at least as fruitful when integrated as when used on their own'

Beside Berg, Hanns Eisler was another member of the inner Schoenberg circle who used *Sprechstimme* writing to good effect. The most significant of Eisler's works of this kind are the *Palmström-Lieder* of 1926 for *Sprechstimme*, flute, clarinet, violin (and viola)

The development of clusters
as shown in (a) Debussy's *Ondine*,
from Book 2 of the *Préludes;*
(b) Cowell's *Tiger;*
(c) Stockhausen's *Gruppen.*

and cello. He also occasionally used the technique in his socialist songs. But a methodical investigation into the links between speech and music had to wait until after 1950. A succession of theories and compositions then appeared, some of which had implications for opera. We shall deal with these later.

The first attempt to use a combination of speech-choruses and a music of pure noise was made by Milhaud in 1915, in his setting of *Les Choéphores* from Claudel's translation of the Oresteia trilogy of Aeschylus. Milhaud calls for mixed speech-choruses accompanied by fifteen percussionists. The fourth, fifth and seventh sections of the work are set for this novel combination alone; the other parts employ solo female voices and a traditional orchestra including four saxophones and four saxhorns.

In 1912, the American composer Henry Cowell added to the range of musical sound-material by introducing note-clusters, groups of ten or more adjacent notes on the piano struck simultaneously. These clusters contain so many closely-packed semitone intervals that the individual note is not registered as such by the ear and contributes only to the impact of the sound as a whole. Note-complexes of this kind can be found in embryo in Debussy's piano music and even in Mussorgsky. Groups of three chromatically-related notes had also been used by Ravel. Note-clusters are not of course to be classed as noises, but nor are they fully-fledged musical shapes in the sense of comprising determinate pitches. Strictly speaking, they are chords built from the smallest possible intervals, whose individual notes play no role in progressions. As against tonal and most non-tonal dissonances, they tend neither to rise nor fall. This static quality and their lack of relation to other chords brings them very close to noises.

But where do musical sounds end and noises begin? This question still remains unanswered, despite countless experiments both after the First World War and after 1945.

Only one composer of standing has dared to make a methodical exploration of the unknown territory first opened up by the Schoenberg school, the bruitists and others: the French composer

Edgard Varèse, who was born in Paris in 1883 and then settled in New York in 1915. After producing a large number of works which made an assault on traditional music without completely breaking with it, Varèse began to compose scores of a wholly novel kind. His youthful works were destroyed by fire in Berlin. His revolutionary American works began with *Hyperprism* (1922–3), a work for small orchestra and percussion. They reached the heights of nonconformity with *Ionisation* (1931), for an ensemble of thirteen percussionists. While working on *Ionisation*, Varèse conceived the idea of a musical laboratory in which experiments could be conducted to discover new methods of using acoustical material. The plan was realised only much later, by Pierre Schaeffer in Paris, but the idea was typical of Varèse's systematic attitude towards his experiments in composition. *Ionisation* is the first major work based on a new conception of music to be dominated by timbre and noise. The composition is organised according to the type of timbre underlined at any point. It is scored for forty instruments, including drums of various sizes, cymbals and wooden drums. Piano and bells, as instruments of definite pitch, are also used. The most interesting and novel effects are caused by the polyphony of *glissandi* of sirens and so-called 'lions' roars' – the first instance of noises being combined with *glissandi* scales, in other words with an infinite number of pitches. *Ionisation* also has a strictly-organised rhythmic and dynamic structure of a type that later became common in the serial works of the Darmstadt school.

Varèse was another composer who met with great hostility from the critics. In 1924 the New York press dismissed *Hyperprism* as the noise of a menagerie or of a factory accident (Olin Downes in the *New York Times*) and Varèse himself as a misguided Schoenbergian. Even *Arcana*, written for the traditional instruments of a large orchestra, met with total incomprehension. It was performed in Berlin in 1932 by Nicholas Slonimsky and the Berlin Philharmonic Orchestra and was described by Paul Schwers, the conservative critic of the influential *Allgemeine Musikzeitung*, as a musical atrocity, insane and barbarous.

Varèse (1885–1965) was a pioneer of 'futuristic' music. In contrast to the linear style of serial composition, his works can be described as agglomerations of rhythms, timbres and dynamics. Noise is also given an organised part in musical form. His work in the thirties in the United States is thus a pre-electronic foretaste of post-war laboratory experiments in Darmstadt and Cologne. Only in very recent years has he been at all widely performed.

The use of noise-producing instruments became a feature of avant-garde music in the twenties and thirties. This was particularly true of French and American composers, but also of Russian and other Slav composers working in America or western Europe. The Schoenberg school remained aloof from and indeed hostile towards such experimentation. Here too Berg took up a position of his own. As early as *Wozzeck*, at the end of the murder scene, he had used the dynamic effect of a prolonged *crescendo* on the note B, and had adopted a form of rhythmic organisation in the subsequent tavern scene. One Western work that used percussion effects as the basis for new methods of composition was George Antheil's *Ballet mécanique*, which caused a sensation when it was performed in 1924. The score calls for ten pianos, and electric instruments and machines, including aeroplane propellers. The straightforward, constant repetition of melodic and rhythmic ideas seeks to create a static music that derives from *Le Sacre du printemps* and is akin to the notions of Varèse. Satie's ballet *Parade* (1917) was a modest precursor of these experiments. Cocteau had suggested that Satie should use sirens, typewriters, aeroplanes and dynamos; Satie settled for sirens and typewriters. Milhaud had called for fifteen percussionists in his ballet *L'Homme et son désir* (1918), and he later wrote a Concerto for percussion and small orchestra (1929–30), as well as various other works using noises. In Alexander Tcherepnin's Symphony in E (1927) there is a scherzo which uses percussion instruments only, in huge polyrhythmic ensembles: castanets, triangle, side drum, tambourine, cymbals, bass drum, tam-tam and stringed instruments, which the players are instructed to strike on the body with the wood of the bow.

4 Simultaneity

Our senses are capable of perceiving and following several different processes at once. This ability can be trained and directed to many practical and artistic ends, in a degree depending partly on the capacities of the individual and partly on cultural and historical conditions. Everything termed polyphony in music is based on it. However, the ability to hear in a polyphonic way is not the same the world over. Some peoples, even at the present day, cannot hear more than one part at a time. In the Arab world there are brilliant musicians who totally reject our polyphonic tradition, because they have been trained historically to hear music in a monophonic way only.

The more man is beset by the technological innovations of the modern world, the more he is compelled to come to terms with a highly complex pattern of sense-perceptions. Social conditions in a modern city militate against the isolation of the individual; at the same time, the isolated sense-impressions of rural life are slowly disappearing. This complex system of perceptions necessarily brings with it a change in artistic attitudes. Various new art-forms have arisen which can be explained and understood only by reference to modern technological city life. The notion of *simultanité* gave a new vision to the generation of painters of 1910. This was most clearly shown in the crystal- or spectrum-like splitting up of optical impressions in the work of futurists such as Gino Severini (e.g. in his picture 'The noise from the street invades the house'), the clashing concrete and abstract forms in Picasso's *Torero*, or the still lives of Braque. We find the notion of simultaneity even in the pictures of Chagall, as for example the famous 'I and the Village', in which impressions of rural life are interlocked and juxtaposed in a highly non-naturalistic fashion. Lyric poetry of the period, particularly of the German expressionists and of Apollinaire, is likewise a poetry of juxtaposed simultaneous perceptions.

European music had used polyphonic techniques for at least a thousand years. Indeed, the early period of polyphony gave rise to a number of unusual phenomena, such as the motets of the later thirteenth century, in which a sacred Latin text with a Gregorian

Braque: 'Guitar and Jug' (1927).
Tate Gallery, London.

melody was frequently combined with two additional parts in the
vernacular using quite different textual and musical procedures.
Separate, simultaneously-sounding strands of this kind presupposed
a trained and highly intelligent audience. In the course of time this
particular species of composition disappeared.

In the modern music of 1910 or thereabouts the principle of
simultaneity was applied in two fields: in tonality and rhythm. In
1908 Bartók wrote the collection of piano pieces entitled *Fourteen
Bagatelles*. The first of these is the earliest thorough-going example
of two simultaneously-sounding melodic parts written in different

Chagall: 'I and the Village'.
Museum of Modern Art, New York.

A motet with three texts
from the period of Petrus de Cruce
(died *circa* 1300).

keys. The technique is graphically illustrated by the allocation of one part to each hand. The right hand plays in four sharps through-out, in C sharp minor. The left hand plays in four flats, in a Phry-gian C minor or modern F minor. The listener is made aware of the fact that the two melodies are in different keys since one is an ascending line, the other descending. As a model of bitonality, then, the piece presents no difficulties to the ear. Other bagatelles in the set, especially the tenth and the thirteenth, also consist of combina-tions of two different tonalities. In the tenth Bartók uses a technique that might be termed 'successive polytonality'. One section of the piece, in which broken chords are combined in a striking way with an upper part, was quoted by Schoenberg in the last chapter of the *Harmonielehre*. The thirteenth bagatelle ('Elle est morte') consists of a hammered ostinato E flat minor triad in the bass and an upper part using the broken triads of D major, G major and so on. How-ever, the piece as a whole has two tonal planes, because the E flat minor ostinato is interrupted from time to time by a similar A minor

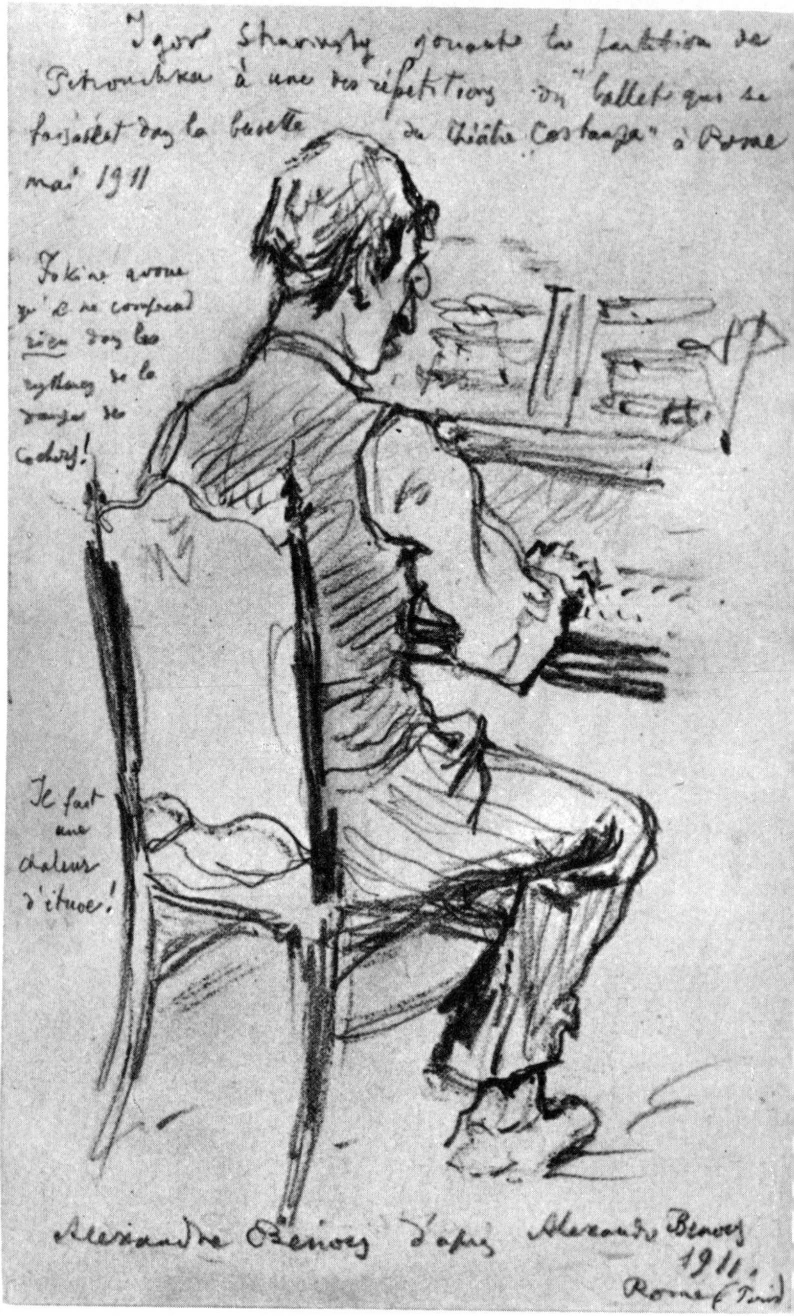

Stravinsky (b. 1882),
drawn by Benois while
rehearsing *Petrushka*.

ostinato, the two tonalities pressing ever closer on each other's heels.

In this piece Bartók combines tonalities which are only very distantly related, including those a tritone apart. This tritone relation is also characteristic of Stravinsky's early uses of bitonality, notably in *Petrushka* (1911). The famous 'Petrushka chord' is a combination of the broken triads of C major and F sharp major. The effect is particularly striking because keys whose tonics lie a tritone apart have the least number of notes in common (e.g. the notes F and B in the case of C major and F sharp major). Sequences of chords a tritone apart are altogether characteristic of Russian music. In the coronation scene in *Boris Godunov* Mussorgsky uses two alternating dominant seventh chords an augmented fourth apart, and Rimsky-Korsakov's fanfares in *Sheherazade* cosist of two minor triads a tritone apart. The tritone relation, incidentally, comes into play in other passages of *Petrushka*: the melody in the Nursemaids' dance, for example, is accompanied throughout by parallel movement at the tritone. And finally, in *Le Sacre du printemps*, tritone harmonies become virtually the norm.

Prokofiev's piano pieces *Sarcasmes* (1911) also contain bitonal passages, and, like Bartók, Prokofiev gives the two systems different key-signatures. Certain passages in Busoni's *Sonatina Seconda* consist of polytonal sequences of triads in contrary motion, with the keys of F major, E major and E flat major set against triads of D major, C major and D flat major.

Composition on more than one tonal plane was prefigured in both Debussy and Richard Strauss. In *Pelléas et Mélisande* and his later piano music, Debussy often writes parallel non-functional chord progressions, in a style very close to the 'successive polytonality' of Bartók. Strauss in the tone-poem *Also sprach Zarathustra* frequently combines the keys of C major and B major; indeed, the work closes with a high pianissimo B major triad, answered by a C in the bass. In *Salome* triads belonging to different tonalities often appear in rapid succession or simultaneously. In the Jews' quintet in the opera D flat major and D minor are brought together through the melodic writing. Similar tendencies can be found in the piano

Milhaud (b. 1892) was with Honegger
the most gifted of 'Les Six'.
He writes in polytonal style and
incorporates jazz elements and
folk-music into many of his works.

music of Scriabin. Hans Newsidler's *Judentanz* of 1535 and Mozart's
Musical Joke may be regarded as early experiments of the same
kind.

Bitonality and polytonality became particularly prevalent in
French and Italian music after 1912. The Italian composer Casella,
who was originally influenced by Strauss and Mahler, composed in
a polytonal style in *Notte di Maggio* (1914) and his Piano Sonatina

of 1916 has a polytonal minuet and a bitonal finale. The American composer Charles Ives, presumably quite independently of like-minded contemporary European composers, also experimented with polytonality in his orchestral and piano music before the First World War.

But the composer to apply most consistently the technique of two or more simultaneously-sounding tonalities was Darius Milhaud. He also dealt with the problem of polytonality from the theoretical angle. In an essay published in the *Musikblätter des Anbruch* in 1924 he cited the second movement of Bach's Italian Concerto, in which B flat major and D minor sound together at one point. He himself produced a particularly attractive example of polytonality in the ballet *Le Boeuf sur le toit* of 1919, in which Brazilian folk-songs and carnival tunes from Rio de Janeiro in two or three, and in one case even four, different tonalities are joined together in a very simple fashion. The music's quirkish charm consists in the fact that only simple tonic, dominant and subdominant cadences are used within each tonal plane, but that when all of them sound together they produce a highly dissonant and novel form of harmony. In this particular instance the effect is similar to the chance combinations of sounds we hear on a fairground when two orchestrions or steam-organs are playing simultaneously in two different keys (the very situation depicted in Stravinsky's *Petrushka*). But apparently simple as his original impulse may have been, Milhaud's later works are extremely subtle. So, for that matter, are the simple major-minor juxtapositions of his *Saudades do Brasil* of 1920–1. Ernst Křenek, who was closely connected with the Schoenberg school, has advanced a critical analysis of Milhaud's highly individual brand of polytonality. According to Křenek, Milhaud wanted to be able to use both a 'progressive', dissonant, atonal musical language, and a diatonic melodic style in complete antithesis to German chromaticism. For this reason, he claims, a justification of Milhaud's technique could be made only on strictly personal, not on theoretical, grounds: most of the works in question cannot be said to be in any definite key. But in point of fact the polytonal music of Milhaud and others consciously exploited a notion of simultaneity, much as did a large number of paintings between 1912 and 1925. In general terms, too, there were very close connections between surrealist art and music written on two or more tonal planes. Polytonality and polymodality are related to atonality as stages in the development of music, except that the two former preserve a sense of the old major and minor modes, even of the church modes, while the chromaticism of the German school deliberately leads away from tonality. The advantage of polytonality is that it still leaves room for stylistic possibilities such as neo-classicism, and music based on folk-song. And bimodality can actually lead to panchromaticism, from a melodic point of view: an ascending Lydian scale and a descending Phrygian scale within the same octave give all the twelve notes, with one note coming twice and another three times. For example:

The principle of simultaneity was brought to bear not only in the fields of melody, harmony and tonality, but in the field of rhythm. Of course, the juxtaposition of several rhythmic planes is *per se* a feature of all advanced polyphony. But there is a difference between the contrapuntal repetition of rhythmic ideas in different melodic parts, and the use of rhythmic figures which are treated and developed quite separately and independently. Mozart's counterpoint is always rhythmically diversified and vital, but the contrasts of rhythm are always subordinated to the wider melodic context. On the other hand, the simultaneous minuet, contredanse and quick waltz of the three bands in the first-act finale of *Don Giovanni* are a deliberate use of polyrhythmic and polymetric writing. In this instance the three strands are intended to be heard as distinct entities, just like the separate tonal planes of polytonal music.

In classical symphonic music there are occasionally passages where several different rhythmic processes are superimposed on one

Polymetrical writing in
the finale to Act 1 of
Mozart's *Don Giovanni*.

81

another. Such instances also produce an effect of polyrhythms. The
ear registers the rhythms as distinct yet conjoined entities. Hermann
Scherchen discussed examples of polyrhythms of this kind from the
first and second movements of Beethoven's First Symphony, using
the terms 'cross-metres' and 'suspension of metre'. In both cases,
though, what we discern is an independent rhythmic impulse
going against the prevailing metre. It is often hard to separate polymetric and polyrhythmic procedures in Western music. If by 'metre'

we mean a regular, evenly-distributed beat, then any disruption of its symmetry is necessarily a matter of rhythm: rhythm being a musical division imposed on the flow of time and only in this sense able to function as an antithesis of metre. The displacement of accents within an overall metre is the product of a rhythmic impulse. If these rhythmic impulses occur in various different parts and are ordered among themselves, the resulting effect is polyrhythmic. The early polyphony of the Middle Ages is rich in polyrhythmic procedures. It was only in later European music that the rhythmic sense became constricted and symmetrical metres became standard.

Polymetric techniques also include frequent changes in time-signature, such as are found in Stravinsky from *Petrushka* onwards, developed to the extreme limit in *Le Sacre du printemps* and brilliantly reduced to the bare bones in *L'Histoire du soldat*. We have already discussed the movement away from rigid symmetrical metres. A constantly-changing time-signature is only one of the ways in which this was achieved. Oddly enough, it is far harder to overcome the effects of musical training with regard to rhythm than with regard to harmony. The law of inertia clearly applies both mentally and physically to someone with a European training. One of the great educational achievements of the Swiss Émile Jaques-Dalcroze was to teach young people to think and feel in different rhythm-patterns simultaneously. Most orchestral players in 1910, for example, found it very hard to play groups of five within a 3/4 or 4/4 metre; this was child's play for those brought up on the Dalcroze method. Ballet dancers who had passed through his hands also had no difficulty in interpreting modern music.

One of the earliest twentieth-century composers to come to grips with polymetric and polyrhythmic writing was Charles Ives, born in 1874, the same year as Schoenberg (whom he survived by three years). In 1904 Ives wrote a piece called *March 1776* which he later incorporated into *Three Places in New England*. In this piece two marches in different tempi are combined in a velocity ratio of 4:3. In Ives' later works all kinds of asymmetrical metres occur, both in succession and simultaneously, and he also uses syncopations and

An excerpt from 'Putnam's Camp', the second
of Ives' *Three Places in New England*.
The trumpet is playing 'The British Grenadiers',
a tune which, curiously, was very popular with
American soldiers in the 1770s and 80s.

shifts of accents within the bar. Numerous examples can be found
in the Fourth Symphony (1916) and the First Piano Sonata (1909);
in the latter, 5/4, 4/4 and 3/4 are used strictly in parallel.

In Satie's *Parade* the Managers have a theme that is metrically
ambivalent. The theme's character changes completely if the accents
are re-arranged. In different metres it can thus play quite different
musical roles. This technique has no connection with Stravinsky's
brand of polyrhythmic writing, though Stravinsky achieved similar
results in *L'Histoire du soldat*, which was composed at the time of
Parade. In many places in this score there are two distinct, parallel
rhythmic planes. The lower plane is an *ostinato* in march rhythm
with strictly regular accents. The upper part superimposed on it is
rhythmically quite independent of the bass and is itself asymmetrical in structure. Since the two parts are always conjoined, the rhythmic accents are in a constant state of flux. The listener is made to

March from Stravinsky's
L'Histoire du soldat showing
the tensions between the two
rhythmic layers of the composition.

feel from time to time that the balanced tread of the march has been disturbed: he suddenly feels that the accents of the underlying rhythm are coming in the wrong place, because the accents of the upper part have imposed themselves more strongly. The effect is precisely analogous to Milhaud's polytonality, which Křenek claimed to be fundamentally non-tonal. In fact, however, it is quite possible to follow musical events occurring on two or more levels at once and to keep the levels themselves separate in one's mind. The polyrhythmic techniques of modern music exploit this fact.

L'Histoire du soldat bears witness to other changes in our sense of rhythm. In the scene with the Princess, for example, at the points of

A typically asymmetrical African folk-tune. It is from West Africa and the words are 'The white man's bird flies all over the world'.

transition between the tango, waltz and ragtime, there are unusual examples of double rhythms; at these points the accents are hardly definable any longer, and the same shifting balance is produced as in the case of the combinations of two rhythmic levels. Stravinsky's music between 1920 and 1950 was noticeably subdued as far as rhythm was concerned, but the ballet *Agon* (1957) marks something of a return to the metrical and rhythmic experimentation of his earlier works, although it is now coupled with serial techniques.

Two important influences on the growth of complex rhythms were ragtime and, more particularly, jazz. Syncopation – non-symmetrical shifts of accent within a symmetrical metre – is in itself a feature of an emancipated sense of rhythm. It derives from the highly subtle rhythms of African music, which had been imported into the New World by negro slaves. Jazz dance-forms are often unmistakably polyrhythmic in character, and their sources have been the subject of recent anthropological research. Rhythms of this kind are prevalent in the songs and dances of central Africa. In 1952 an Englishman, Kenneth R. Long, published a children's song of the Ndebele, a Bantu tribe, which in linear terms alone reveals a wealth of rhythmic tensions, with alternations of 7/8, 3/8, 7/8, 3/8, 3/4, 5/8 and so on. Added to it, however, is a rhythmic accompaniment, the accents of which only partly coincide with those of the melody. Ragtime and jazz have had to hold their own in European surroundings and they therefore conform to our symmetrical metres. But they manage to combine with them all their original rich alternating rhythms, which result in rhythmic processes on two or three different levels. Melodic figures play an important role by exploiting rhythmic subdivisions going against the beat. Cross-rhythms, such as 6/8 against 3/4, are also found in the folk-dances of various European countries. The *polo* of Andalusia is in 3/8 but changes into 3/4 when the last semiquaver of one bar is joined by a hemiola rhythm to the first semiquaver of the next. The *furiant* of Bohemia is a similar case. Conversely, there are *Ländler* forms in Bavaria, the so-called *Schuhplattler*, which have clearly defined 3/8 melodies within an overall 3/4 metre. Alfred Baresel, in his book on rhythm in jazz and dance music, gives various examples of native African drum rhythms. Two drums, for instance, play together in a duet, one in strict 3/4 and the other in 4/4. Diminution of the counter-rhythm into quavers produces the rhythms characteristic of the advanced jazz style known as swing (though they can also be found in early blues). Writers on jazz, such as Joachim Ernst Berendt, have often pointed out the relationship between jazz and baroque music, drawing analogies between the melodic multiplicity of Bach and the rhythmic multiplicity of jazz. Although Western art-music became increasingly impoverished as regards metre from the sixteenth century onwards, all the great composers clearly have had a rhythmic sense which, as it were, transcended metrical rules. Combinations of different rhythm patterns, known in Italian late-baroque music as *imbroglio*, preserved a modest existence in romantic music. Counter-rhythms are found occasionally in Chopin's dances; for example, Baresel quotes the piece *Des Abends* from Schumann's *Fantasiestücke* as an instance of polyrhythm, in which a hemiola rhythm leads to a clashing of accents between the upper and lower parts. There is also an *imbroglio* at the end of the second-act finale of *Die Meistersinger*.

But while such instances have been exceptional in European classical and romantic music, in jazz and some modern art-music they have become the rule. It is highly probable that the centuries-old habit of thinking in terms of symmetrically-recurring accents has been weakening since the beginning of the twentieth century. In its stead has come a richer, more complex sense of rhythm, which has so far not been exploited to any great degree in modern works. This explains the interest, often the fascination, that many musicians have shown in their encounters with jazz. The polyrhythms we observed in *L'Histoire du soldat* would have been unthinkable but for the jazz records which Ansermet brought Stravinsky from America during the First World War. There is after all a fundamental difference between the constantly changing metres of *Le Sacre du printemps* and the double levels of rhythm of *L'Histoire du soldat*. Ragtime and jazz have left their traces in art-music, particularly French music, since 1910. After the First World War many avant-garde composers were evidently much under the influence of jazz-style rhythms. They included not only Stravinsky and Hindemith, but countless composers from France, England and Italy.

In the main, German composers, firmly bound as they were by a sense of tradition, remained untouched by jazz. Yet even Richard Strauss, a traditionalist for all his modernisms, found his own way to polyrhythms, and used them in tone-poems such as *Don Quixote* (1898). There are also passages in *Salome*, for example the quartet between Herod, Herodias, Salome and the voice of Jochanaan, where two metres are heard at once, 3/4 and 2/4, and later 4/4 and 5/4. When Strauss at the height of his career half-jokingly said that a good conductor does not need a left hand, he was forgetting what he had expected of conductors in his youth. In polymetric and polyrhythmic music the performer has to carry out more than one operation simultaneously. A conductor has to make his beats quite distinct and separate, which means in practice that his left hand must be independent of his right. Of the various followers of Schoenberg, Berg was the most open to the use of rhythm as a means of construction. Schoenberg himself also came close to the complex rhythmic writing of Stravinsky and Bartók in some works of the twenties. The last movement of the *Serenade* (1921–4), for example, has a passage which is isorhythmic in the fourteenth-century sense: themes and motifs are subordinated to a purely rhythmic idea. Berg quite independently composed the tavern scene in Act 3 of *Wozzeck* as an 'invention on a rhythm'; the scene is marked by polyrhythmic techniques which stem from Berg's general mode of thinking in terms of several different musical levels at once. The last movement of the Chamber Concerto for piano, violin and thirteen wind instruments (1923–5) is even more complicated. The intellectual virtuosity of the work as a whole makes it one of the most astonishing products of modern art. It combines purely private and personal details, such as the musical treatment of the names 'Arnold Schoenberg', 'Anton Webern' and 'Alban Berg', with the most ingenious techniques of classical and modern composition. The first two movements are a *Thema scherzoso con variazioni*, for piano and wind, and an *Adagio* for violin and wind; the third movement Berg calls *Rondo ritmico con introduzione*, for piano, violin and wind. Berg made an analysis of the work in a letter to Schoenberg, for whose fiftieth birthday the work was planned (though it was not finished in time):

Finally, the third movement is a fusion of the two preceding. . . . There were really three main methods of combining movements I and II: firstly, free counterpointing of corresponding parts; secondly, successive juxtaposition in a kind of duet of particular phrases and small sections, repeated note for note from the earlier movements; and thirdly, adding together exactly whole passages from both movements.

Adding together exactly—what is this but 'simultaneity' once more, as the term has been used in modern painting? Two musical processes, self-sufficient and fully developed in themselves, are combined and unfold simultaneously. The principle is no different from that *imbroglio* in *Don Giovanni* when Mozart simultaneously depicts three levels of eighteenth-century society. In the process, however, Berg creates a form, modestly named 'Rondo ritmico', which is in fact something entirely new. The movement contains three important rhythmic elements: a 'principal' and a 'subsidiary' rhythm, and a smaller purely motivic idea. These rhythms serve to reshape the themes and they are also combined in polyrhythmic fashion, inasmuch as the frequently changing metres of the Rondo are a combination of the 6/4 of the Variations and the *alla breve* of the Adagio. The fact that, on top of all this, a piano-concerto movement and violin-concerto movement are combined to form a double concerto, adds immeasurably to the fascination of the finale.

Berg had further recourse to techniques of this kind in his Violin Concerto (1935) and the unfinished opera *Lulu*. These and other works show him to have been one of the earliest European composers to enrich and co-ordinate every aspect of the craft of composition. His music is as much governed by the notion of simultaneity as are some of the major paintings of Max Ernst, the Futurists or Picasso. Its astonishing blend of free-roving imagination and strict compliance with rules points far into the future.

5 New means of organisation

It is hard to endure absolute freedom. This sorry truth applies not only to society but to every form of intellectual activity. A state of affairs in which all choices are open because no laws exist or are acknowledged militates against artistic creativity. Artistic forms are dictated solely by the feelings; a line between coherence and incoherence cannot be drawn.

In the first years of the twentieth century, existing musical conventions were thrown overboard in a revolt of the collective unconscious. Tonality, harmony, melody and rhythm broke away from the consensus that had governed Western music for centuries. What had seemed sacrosanct proved to be transitory; eternal laws were revoked with relative ease. As happens in every sphere, almost limitless freedom led to a state of uncertainty. A composer faced with a boundless supply of sonorities and rhythm-patterns, not to mention the little-explored realm of noises, will inevitably tend towards anarchism. If he has not unconsciously inherited a sense of tradition, he may be led into dangerous confusion. This threat had been hanging over music since *Tristan*, with the weakening of tonality implied by Wagner's harmonic writing. If we use the word 'crisis' in its strict sense, as relating to turning-points and moments of decision, then music entered a state of crisis in 1908. Tonality no longer existed, and this set the seal on the break-up of organised law. Psychologically speaking, the complete sovereignty of the emotions that superseded musical laws was a case of over-compensation. The very feature that had marked out creative artists since the turn of the century – their intellectuality – now collided with a counter-force of an astonishing kind. It is the tension of this situation that gives the works of art of about 1910 their peculiar power. This period lasted only a short time, however: it was a fleeting episode within the broad flow of history. The first non-representational pictures of Kandinsky, the lyric poems of August Stramm, Schoenberg's George *Lieder* and his monodrama *Erwartung*, and the works of Schoenberg's pupils, were evidence of a new spirit in art and life. But it was not possible to dwell for long in the highly-charged atmosphere of this expressionist surge of feeling.

The first searches for new means of organisation took the form of a purely instinctive adherence to certain laws or principles of composition. In *Erwartung*, despite the thorough-going athematicism, repetitions of tiny motivic cells, such as the three-note complex D-F-C sharp, were permitted. Schoenberg, Berg and Webern also used *ostinato* rhythmic and melodic figures. The polymetric and polyrhythmic techniques of Stravinsky's *Le Sacre du printemps* can similarly be reduced to a few recurring formulae.

Free pan-chromaticism, or non-tonal harmonic and melodic writing, tended to entail, even in Reger and Debussy, the unwritten rule that notes should never or only rarely be repeated. Bans on repetition had already been found in tonal music and in music based on the church modes. They are a feature of any highly-developed compositional technique and spring from a felt need for balance. In the case of a musical language that was progressing from seven-note diatonicism to twelve-note chromaticism, hostility to repetition had an easily predictable end-result: melodic or chordal shapes in which each of the twelve semitones appeared once and once only. Among Schoenberg's followers shapes of this kind were occasionally used even in works written in an extended tonality, as for example in Berg's *Altenberg Lieder*, which contain a twelve-note chord and a twelve-note melody.

As we have seen, twelve-note melodies and chord-progressions had previously occurred. But when they did, even in Strauss's 'Wissenschaft' fugue from *Also sprach Zarathustra*, they figured in a tonal context. They were foreign bodies, as it were, integrated into an already intact musical language. In the New Viennese School these tonal ties disappeared. Pan-chromatic ideas were no longer used as exceptional or special cases but as the elements of a new system of relations not yet governed by rules. Indeed, in this sense the Viennese composer Josef Matthias Hauer (1883–1959) probably wrote 'purely atonal melodies' before Schoenberg and his pupils. The earliest of them date from piano pieces of 1914. The pieces, in fact, are complete forms built up from purely atonal melodies of this kind. Hauer described his aims in a text-book on atonal music.

entitled *On the Nature of Music*, which was published in 1920. He starts from a notion of 'equal temperament', that is, a chromatic technique which uses mathematical procedures to combat the tendency of a tonic to become established. He characterises the music he advocates as follows:

In atonal music, however, which stems from 'totalities', intervals alone are relevant. Musical expression is no longer achieved through the use of major and minor keys and of specific instruments with a *single* timbre: it is founded on the totality of intervals and timbres, and this is best and most clearly realised by using one single, tempered instrument.

He says further on:

The 'law' or 'nomos' [of atonal music] is that *all twelve notes* of the temperament are to be repeated over and over again.

Undoubtedly Hauer preceded the Schoenberg school in calling for and employing all twelve notes of the melos. However, the idea was certainly in the air at the time.

Schoenberg was the first to realise the dangers of the complete freedom he had inaugurated. His attempt in *Pierrot Lunaire* (1912) to infuse traditional forms into the new non-tonal language gave rise to such brilliant yet strange creations as the passacaglia *Nacht* and the fugues and mirror canons of *Der Mondfleck*. However, this was in effect a purely personal compromise that clearly failed to satisfy him. At all events he did not repeat the experiment until 1923. During the First World War he completed only the Four Songs with Orchestra Op. 22, which are formally free in construction. He was, however, engaged on various compositions which were to remain at the draft stage or were never finished. One such attempt was the uncompleted symphony mentioned in a letter to Nicolas Slonimsky of 3 June 1937. In the letter Schoenberg states that the symphony's scherzo, which was sketched in late 1914 and early 1915, was built on a twelve-note theme, though other themes were used in the rest of the work. The oratorio *Die Jakobsleiter*, which has links with the music of the symphony, contains two six-note themes which

The series of Schoenberg's third Song Op. 48. This is unique in that the notes of each hexachord form a whole-tone scale.

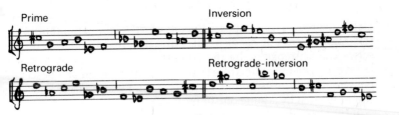

together form a twelve-note series. In the same letter Schoenberg says:

> My *conscious* aim was always to build up my musical structures from one unifying idea which was the source of all the other ideas and also governed the accompaniment and chords, or the 'harmonies'. I made many attempts to achieve this. But very few of them were completed or published.

Schoenberg mentions his Piano Pieces Op. 23 and the Serenade Op. 24 as such attempts. But it was not until the Piano Suite Op. 25, work on which began in the summer of 1921, that the method of composition we know as twelve-note technique was consistently applied for the first time.

Schoenberg himself spoke of the method in rather roundabout fashion as 'composition with twelve notes related only to one another'. Every work composed in this way is built on a series or basic idea (*Grundgestalt*) in which the twelve notes appear in a determinate, unchanging order. Thus far the musical material corresponds to Hauer's 'purely atonal melodies'. But whereas in Hauer's case different melodies of this kind can be combined quite freely, in Schoenberg's case the series is the sole source of musical material in the work in question and so constitutes its actual substance. The compositional technique involved consists of using the three mirror forms of the basis series: the retrograde (the notes in reverse order), inversion (reversed direction of the intervals) and retrograde inversion (the two combined). This raises the number of twelve-note series available to four. Each can then be transposed on to the other eleven degrees. The composer thus has forty-eight permutations of the original series at his disposal. Furthermore, any interval of the series can be replaced by the complementary interval within the octave, e.g. an ascending fourth by a descending fifth, or a descending semitone by an ascending major seventh. Finally, larger intervals can be created by adding one or more octaves.

It is clear that this new twelve-note method of organisation rescued music from the tempting dangers of the freedom it had so recently gained. Indeed, the new rules were stricter than the old rules of tonality. They are comparable for strictness with advanced canonic techniques, from which, after all, their own mirror techniques were derived. Of these mirror forms, the inversion is most easily discernible by the ear. The retrograde requires careful attention on the part of the listener and a certain amount of intellectual effort. Schoenberg himself used an illustration to defend the use of mirror techniques. A hat, he said, remains a hat, whether it is seen from above or below, or from the side or from in front. Whether, however, all listeners can hear a twelve-note series as clearly as they can see a hat, Schoenberg's jocular analogy does not say.

In the early twenties, when the first twelve-note compositions appeared, there were many other signs of a search for new means of organisation. There was a sharp and striking division between those composers who had been brought up in the Austrian tradition and those of other European backgrounds. Vienna was to remain for a long time the focal point of all endeavours to find new substitutes for melodic and harmonic organisation. After 1924 Schoenberg's pupils followed him in adopting twelve-note composition: Webern in the Three Folk Texts Op. 17 for voice, violin (and viola), clarinet and bass-clarinet, Berg in the Chamber Concerto for piano, violin and thirteen wind instruments, and Eisler in the *Palmström Lieder* for *Sprechstimme*, flute (and piccolo), clarinet, violin (and viola) and cello. All three composers give the method their own characteristic stamp. In Webern's Folk Texts twelve-note melodic and chordal complexes create a kind of mosaic. The series and its mirror forms are segmented, and a functional role is played by a kind of varied *ostinato*. Berg uses twelve-note complexes alongside free passages in an extended or suspended tonality, and he also uses forms of rhythmic organisation similar to those in *Wozzeck*. Eisler uses the method for the purposes of ironic melodrama in the style of *Pierrot Lunaire*. In their later works Berg and, more especially, Webern showed how diversified the applications of the new technique could be. Hauer had already singled out certain basic types from among the vast number of possible twelve-note permutations and listed them as forty-four 'tropes'. He divided twelve-note melodies into two six-note halves standing in given symmetry-relations to each other. Berg experimented with so-called 'all-interval' series, using them in a setting of a poem by Theodor Storm and in the Lyric Suite for string quartet. A pupil of his, F. H. Klein, devoted special attention to all-interval series, one of which yields the so-called 'mother chord' consisting of twelve different notes and eleven different intervals. Webern, on the other hand, favoured series with only a few different intervals. The most interesting series of this type is that of the Concerto for nine instruments Op. 24 (1934), which can be reduced to the three-note figure

The three mirror forms, each transposed, make up the twelve-note series:

(retrograde inversion, retrograde and inversion). Each of the four groups consists of a semitone and a major third. This not only makes for a drastically simplified compositional style but also eases the task of listening, because only a single three-note idea and its mirror forms have to be identified.

Schoenberg also had a preference for particular types of series. He set most store by those whose inversion at the lower fifth could act as the accompaniment for thematic ideas based on the original series, without note-repetitions in corresponding halves of either series. Berg in his last works made further experiments with twelve-note series. His Violin Concerto (1935) uses a quasi-tonal series composed of sequences of triads, which enabled him to use polytonal techniques:

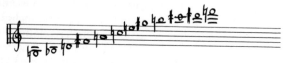

(G minor and A minor, D major and E major triads, the augmented triads B flat – D – F sharp and C – E – G sharp, the diminished triad F sharp – A – C, and a sequence of whole tones.) In *Lulu*, his last, unfinished work, the final act of which was completed only in short score, Berg expands his material by performing mathematical operations on the series. The series consists of the notes:

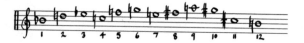

A second series is obtained by taking every seventh note of the original series:

A third series is produced by taking every fifth note:

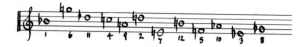

These three different series are used as *Leitthemen*, as it were, each being allocated to a particular character in the opera. Berg also derives four three-part chords from the original series and assigns them as a motif to the central character of Lulu. By using other techniques of his own invention he obtains the remaining motivic and chordal material from the original series. The result is a highly strict piece of musical organisation. Admittedly, the listener cannot recognise it as such on first hearing. He can understand the music only by examining the score and closely studying its structure. But that in no way vitiates the work's artistic quality. The same applies to all complicated forms of polyphony, notably Netherlands Renaissance polyphony, which likewise cannot immediately be understood unless the listener is thoroughly acquainted with the formal techniques involved. A genuine work of art has several different levels of significance, and evokes responses at different levels of awareness. A highly complicated Bach fugue follows a harmonic design which can be grasped quite intuitively. The subtlest twelve-tone construction would be mere empty mathematics if the composer did not imbue it with life on levels that are immediately accessible to the listener. Berg's music in particular, *Lulu* especially, is notable for the immediate impression it makes on the unsophisticated listener. Berg himself said à propos of *Wozzeck* that his chief aim in his operas was just this immediate emotional impact on the audience.

With Vienna, Paris had been the chief centre for new ventures in composition since before the First World War. But while German and Austrian music had unremittingly followed the path of chromaticism and the dissolution of diatonicism and tonality, in France quite different traditions prevailed. Rhythmic elements had always played a greater part in French music, with its roots in dance-forms. In this respect French music was more akin to Russian and Balkan music. In France, moreover, a modal melodic style going back to the church modes had never been completely ousted by major-minor tonality. This adherence to modality prevented French music from being swamped by a tidal wave of chromaticism. Even the most complex harmonies of Debussy and Ravel retain a diatonic basis, and their melodic writing is never completely chromaticised. True, the influence of Wagner had left its mark on French music in the last third of the nineteenth century, decisively so in a few cases. But the modal feeling was merely dormant.

A reaction against German romanticism, particularly against Wagner, had already set in by the turn of the century. In this Satie was a key figure. It was he who roused Debussy to rebel against the hegemony of Wagner and gave him constant encouragement. Indeed, Satie's piano pieces of the late eighties, the *Sarabandes* and *Gymnopédies*, at once primitive and sophisticated, contained the seeds of all that was to figure under the collective term of 'neoclassicism' almost forty years later.

The First World War saw a strengthening of anti-romanticist forces in France. They were assisted by a revival of national feeling, which was most clearly expressed by the appellation of 'Musicien français' under which Debussy wrote his last sonatas. The aesthetic programme of 'Les Six', who made their first public appearance as a group in Paris at the beginning of 1920, was strongly anti-romanticist in tone. Jean Cocteau had already dissociated modern French art from Wagner, the symbol of German music, in his manifesto *Le Coq et L'Arlequin* (1918). But he also emphasised its dissociation from Schoenberg: '. . . all our musicians and Stravinsky owe something to him, but Schoenberg is first and foremost a blackboard musician'. Not content with this. Cocteau also expressed reservations about Debussy, undisguisedly preferring Satie, particularly the Satie of *Parade*. The manifesto was dedicated to the youngest member of the subsequent 'Six' group, Georges Auric. In 1918 Auric was one of a small circle of musicians calling themselves 'Les nouveaux jeunes' whom Satie had taken under his wing. Besides Auric, the group included Artur Honegger, Francis Poulenc, Roland-Manuel and Germaine Tailleferre. Roland-Manuel was the only one of these who did not become a member of 'Les Six'; Louis Durey, and Milhaud, who returned from Brazil in 1919, completed the later group. A few months after the first concert of works by

Satie (1866–1925),
drawn by Cocteau.

'Les Six', Diaghilev's Russian Ballet staged Stravinsky's *Pulcinella* at the Paris Opera. This is a one-act work with vocal items based on themes by Pergolesi, and is composed as a suite, with classical dances such as the gavotte and minuet. Stravinsky uses the classical material in a manner both innovatory and conservative. He largely dispenses with chromatic writing and uses a system of relating degrees of the scale and chords which was to become known as pandiatonicism. The work as a whole made a strong impact as a clean break with romanticism and impressionism. Indeed, it marked a change in Stravinsky's own previous style from *Petrushka* to

'Les Six', painted by Jacques-Émile Blanche. Italics indicate
a member of the group. From left to right: *Germaine Tailleferre*,
Milhaud, *Honegger*, Wiener the pianist and jazz player
Marcelle Meyer (one of the first interpreters of the piano music
of Les Six), *Poulenc*, *Auric* and Cocteau. The missing member of
the group is *Durey*. Picture in the Musèe des Beaux-Arts, Rouen.

L'Histoire du soldat. Rhythmic and metrical innovations are used
very sparingly and polytonal passages are equally rare. This work,
and the Octet for wind of 1923, are clear expressions of the classicist
goal. There had been anticipations of it in Ravel's *Le Tombeau de
Couperin* (1914–7), with its forlane, rigaudon and minuet, and in the
sharp lean style of Satie's *Socrate* of 1919.

Classicism in all these cases was a reaction from a surfeit of misty
impressionist sonorities. Rich colours were replaced by precise lines.
The chief stylistic influence in Stravinsky's Octet is Bach, with ad-
mixtures of Rossinian *buffo*. The return to the eighteenth century is
significant. It abruptly dispelled the disquiet that was induced by
other modern music – here were the chords of the harmony books.
However, they are no longer joined in peaceful progressions, but
are removed from their usual context, intermingle and become
something almost new and untouched. Stravinsky's new style is diatonic, but in a special sense: the notes of the major and minor scale
are registered only in their totality and can be superimposed on each
other at will. Chords built on thirds or fourths are found alongside
clusters of notes and purely melodic lines that are combined in a
web of free-moving polyphony. Tonic and dominant chords no
longer stand in the relation of tension and release, since they occur
simultaneously. Tonalities are merged in similar fashion, not as the
result of a subtle process of chord-blending, but coupled in the
mock-naive style that had been elaborated by Milhaud into a special
technique.

In about 1920 there was a parting of the ways between the two
movements that were attempting to enrich and revitalise musical
language. Twelve-tone technique entailed the composer's subjection
to the growing autonomy of the musical material; Neo-classicism
attempted to invoke the magical power of familiar forms, even if
only in the borrowed robes of an earlier age. Neither was intended
by their creators as a call to revolution. Both laid claim to a con-
servatism which public opinion hotly disputed.

Post-romantic music, free atonality, and even Schoenberg's early
twelve-note music compositions sought to achieve subtle shadings

and nuances in melody, harmony and rhythm. Stravinsky's early neo-classical music, on the other hand, dispensed with shadings altogether. This is illustrated most clearly by the dynamic markings of the Octet, in which *crescendi* and *diminuendi* disappear and only *forte* and *piano* are used. It is a reinstatement of the Baroque technique of a terraced dynamics, which acts, however, not as a courtly aristocratic mannerism but as a source of shock, with sudden outbursts and unexpected silences.

At the end of the Octet is a fugato, the earliest in the works of Stravinsky's maturity. It is really a quasi-fugato, a conscious gesture towards a form whose beauty can still be recognised and imitated but whose content is no longer taken as meaningful. Stravinsky subsequently wrote several fugues of this type. The best-known example is the double fugue from the *Symphony of Psalms* (1930), where the free linear part-writing in choir and orchestra generates extremes of grating dissonance. Against Stravinsky's will, as it were, Neo-classicism was proving to have revolutionary traits. From the time of Reger, the fugue had been used as a vehicle of free chromatic accumulation; this development was now abruptly cut short.

Schoenberg recognised the revolutionary import of ideas he could only condemn. His Three Satires for Mixed Chorus Op. 28 (1925–6) are directed against Stravinsky and other contemporary composers. In the third of the satires, the cantata *Der neue Klassizismus*, he pointedly combines a descending C major scale with a rising pentatonic figure 'on the black keys' to form a twelve-note complex. Certainly, there were plenty of musical nonentities who took their cue from early Stravinskian Neo-classicism, but much valuable chamber music was written as well, by Hindemith, Honegger and Milhaud. Stravinsky himself moved on to the monumental *Oedipus Rex* and the transparent concertante textures of the *Dumbarton Oaks* concerto, with its genuine homage to Bach. Important stages further along his path were marked by the two symphonies (the Symphony in C of 1940 and the Symphony in Three Movements of 1946), the ballet *Orpheus* and finally, the opera *The Rake's Progress*, in which the ghosts of opera buffa and opera seria converse in a

'Abstract Composition 1912', by Kandinsky.
Marlborough Fine Art Gallery, London.

language of half-quotations and esoteric allusions.

Long before Stravinsky and the French neo-classicists, the way back to Bach had been indicated by Busoni. His *Fantasia Contrappuntistica* (completed in 1912), a gigantic attempt to complete Bach's *Art of Fugue*, is admittedly rooted in romantic harmony. Occasionally however, at critical formal points, it points towards a new concept of harmony that is in its own way polytonal. In 1920 Busoni issued his first explicit call for a 'young classicism'. In a letter to the critic Paul Bekker he demanded that 'the results of all earlier experiments should be classified, exploited and mastered, and should be converted into lasting, beautiful forms'. He called for a 'departure from thematicism and the reinstatement of melody as the governing principle of part-writing and musical movement, and as the source and bearer of inspiration and harmony: in short, a return to the highest forms of polyphony!' And he appealed to composers to 'abandon subjectivism and recapture the serenity of absolute music'.

When Cocteau heard Stravinsky's Russian-cum-classicist comedy *Mavra* in 1922, he was put in mind of something 'balancing on the edge of the void'. He spoke of clowns playing the mandolin on top of a pile of balancing chairs. This picture brings out the affinities between Busoni's 'recaptured serenity' and the music of Satie, whose fairground music in *Parade* was no different in essentials from the music he wrote for the last conversation of the dying Socrates. All his life Satie had set his sights on a *musique depouillée*, from the mystical chords of the *Messe des pauvres*, by way of the *Sarabandes*, *Gymnopédies* and *Gnossiennes*, to the ironic piano pieces, the popular dances of *Parade* and the *Trois pieces montées* for orchestra. With him French anti-romanticism entered a phase of asceticism and sarcastic mockery of the emotions. In *Socrate* (1919) lush orchestral sonorities are completely rejected; its archaic parallel fourths and fifths, rigid *ostinati* and compact thematic periods are gaunt even beneath their affected gauntness. The music produces a static effect, but in a manner wholly different from the immobile, drawn-out sonorities of Debussy, or the criss-cross webs of chromaticism of

Ravel which, oddly, are nonetheless often bound to the steps of the scale. With typical neo-classicist paradox, Satie described *Socrate* as a 'drame symphonique': the work is neither symphonic nor a drama. The term, though, was later to stimulate Stravinsky: *Oedipus Rex* (1927) was something of a delayed response to *Socrate* and was a full working-out of the aesthetic programme for which Satie had provided the blueprint.

The history of German-Austrian classical music is a story of accumulating thematic capital. French and Italian music, to the extent that they were influenced by the German-Austrian tradition, followed this development. The expansion of thematic material was a gradual process. Classical sonata form in C. P. E. Bach and Haydn made do with two themes of contrasting character. From the dialogue between them—from the dialectical synthesis of their 'male-female' opposites, so to speak – there grew the central development or working-out section. From Beethoven to Bruckner the number of themes rose to four and themes themselves were extended to form thematic groups. At the same time, particularly in Brahms, the working-out section became increasingly the main part of the sonata movement, or a summary in microcosm of the whole compositional process. The next stage was full-scale polythematicism. In Mahler, Strauss and early Schoenberg the wealth of musical ideas, of the 'thematic material', led to a degree of structural complexity that severely tested the capacity of the listener.

Neo-classicism took the form of a protest against, and a means of checking, this formal expansion. Two, three, four or countless themes gave way to mono-thematicism. Forms were to grow out of a single idea, as in baroque music. The prescription of the medieval ecclesiastical composers, *plures ex una*, gained a new significance. Even baroque forms, particularly the concerto grosso, became current once more, almost obligatory; so did early simple sonata schemes without a complex working-out section. Debussy's sonatas written during the First World War were an expression of this new simplicity. Young French composers after 1918 instinctively took them as their models. The chamber music of Milhaud and

Poulenc and the simpler compositions of Auric should be heard in this way. Even Honegger, the only one in this group who did not fully concur with its anti-romantic philosophy and stayed loyal to Wagner, wrote music in a simplified, early-classical manner in the early twenties. The baroque suite with its simple collection of dances, which had degenerated into the 'character suite' in the nineteenth century, came into its own once more. The new suite forms also found room for the modern dances that had made their impact on the rhythms of contemporary music: the ragtime, cake-walk, fox-trot and tango. The prototype of all modern suites of this kind was Stravinsky's *L'Histoire du soldat*. The links between the neo-classicist creed of simplification and the revival of French national feeling were pointed out by the Belgian critic Paul Collaer in a short résumé of modern musical styles published in 1925.

This retrospective trend and the return to classical and baroque music was not restricted to France. There was a similar movement in Germany centring round the European figure of Busoni. In his opera *Arlecchino* (1916), in the late piano sonatinas and the piano Toccata, Busoni replied to his own call for a 'young classicism'. His ideas encouraged some younger German and Austrian composers. Hindemith, for example, wrote a series of sonatas for one or two instruments between 1920 and 1923 which were akin to contemporary French music in form and style. His Piano Suite (1922) uses American dance rhythms within a baroque framework. The concerto works Opus 36, Opus 38 and Opus 41 are written in the spirit of the Baroque solo concerto and concerto grosso. The Viennese composer Ernst Křenek, although close to the Schoenberg school and to his teacher Franz Schreker, also began to write concerti grossi in the twenties, such as the Concerti Grossi Op. 10 for six solo instruments and orchestra (1921) and Opus 25, and the Concertino Op. 27 for flute, violin, harpsichord and strings. He also composed a Toccata and Chaconne on a Chorale for piano, and a suite of dances on the same theme.

Re-awakening interest in folk-music also stimulated efforts to create new and simplified means of organisation. Important composers such as Bartók and Kódaly, Falla, Szymanowski and Janaček used folk-dances and folk-songs, not as thematic material, but as models for their own thematic invention. Bartók's Suite for piano (1916) and Dance Suite for orchestra (1923), Falla's *Three-cornered Hat* and Janaček's *Sinfonietta* are sophisticated modernistic examples of this kind. The French composer most receptive to a variety of folk-influences was Milhaud. His encounter with Brazilian folk-music in particular left many traces in his music after 1918, notably in *Saudades do Brasil* and the ballet *Le Boeuf sur le toit*. Milhaud frequently gathers together neo-classical forms, themes coloured by folk-music, and complicated polytonal writing into a harmonic synthesis that approaches the pan-chromaticism of the Viennese school.

Cross-currents and overlappings of this kind are characteristic of the music written between 1918 and 1930. Indeed, the early twelve-note pieces of Schoenberg, the waltz from Opus 23 and the Piano Suite Op. 25, are closer to neo-classicism in their attitude to form than Schoenberg himself would have granted. Even the four movements of the Wind Quintet Op. 26, one of the strictest early twelve-note compositions, follow the classical pattern of first-movement sonata form, scherzo and trio, rondo and so on. Similarly, Berg's Chamber Concerto (1924) relates the baroque concerto grosso form.

Indeed, the similarities go further. We saw that the most important formal trend in Neo-classicism was the reduction of all material to a single musical idea: the thematic over-abundance of Bruckner, Mahler and early Schoenberg was replaced by monothematicism. But this is amazingly in line with twelve-note technique. Schoenberg's doctrine that all elements of a composition are to be derived from a single series is equally a doctrine of monothematicism. This is the very point which distinguishes Schoenberg's serial composition and that of his followers from the twelve-note music of Hauer. Hauer lumps together a potentially unlimited number of twelve-note melodies into larger forms. Schoenberg is intent on the strictest integration and coherence, which he guarantees by mirror forms, transpositions and chord-formations based on the series.

The full resources of the notion of classicism have not yet been tapped. It is a notion that has gone through many transformations since 1920. It embraces at one extreme Schoenberg's twelve-note forms up to the Suite Op. 29, with its odd twelve-note variations on the romantic folk-song *Ännchen von Tharau*, and has enjoyed at the other a charming if illicit liaison with surrealism (compare the early paintings of Chirico, the collages of Max Ernst and the mature works of Salvador Dali). Significantly, the offspring of this latter *mésalliance* were mostly stage works, such as Poulenc's *Les Mamelles de Tirésias* and Virgil Thomson's *Four Saints in Three Acts*.

Although classicism was first conceived and shaped in the Latin countries, composers in these countries today stand poles apart from its whole aesthetic. Contemporary music in France and Italy, for all its intellectuality, now centres round the emotional and expressive preoccupations of Dallapiccola and Messiaen. There have, however, been some attempts to establish connections between classicism and certain of the doctrines and assumptions of contemporary music.

6 Revisions and reversions

In 1908 the sociologist Sorel cast doubts on the notion of progress, called by him 'the magic word of the nineteenth century'. Disbelief in an unceasing advance in all spheres of human knowledge and civilisation was nothing new. Rousseau had already questioned whether the concept of progress could be applied in the purely intellectual sphere. The history of the arts shows that values do not always improve with the passage of time. We cannot seriously say that the music of the classical period is better than that of the baroque period or that thorough-bass monody is superior to Netherlands polyphony. True, we can speak of enrichments in artistic language, but these enrichments are always bought at the expense of other linguistic elements. The development of European polyphony was a cultural achievement of the highest order, but it went hand in hand with an impoverishment of rhythm and metre. Romantic harmony after Wagner was accompanied by a neglect of contrapuntal techniques. Nineteenth-century innovations in the field of orchestral colour, brought about by the invention of the valve horn, the valve trumpet and other instruments, militated against the sharp delineation of musical ideas. Yet aestheticians of the nineteenth century evolved a theory of progress which survived well into the modern period. One solitary voice went unheeded: that of the Belgian composer and musicologist François-Josephe Fétis, who said in 1830: 'l'art ne progresse pas, il transforme'. Fétis knew something of non-European music, which he recognised as equal in status to European music, and this fortified his conclusions.

The belief in musical progress was given greatest impetus by the theories of Wagner, who believed that his *Gesamtkunstwerk* had superseded all earlier phases of artistic development and made them redundant. Doubtless the intellectualisation of the creative process was an advance on methods which relied on mere vague intuition. In 1847 Wagner wrote to Hanslick, later to be his dreaded critic:

Do not underestimate the power of the intellect; the work of art produced non-consciously belongs to ages far removed from our own: the work of art belonging to an age of the highest civilisation can be the product only of the consciousness.

Strauss's *Rosenkavalier:*
traditional beauty and grace return
to modern music, an example of
a composer's 'revisionism'.

But what Wagner and his supporters failed to recognise, both then and later, was that composers might continue to produce works without recourse to a naive romantic faith in progress. Verdi's best Italian operas were written within the framework of a national tradition that tolerated basic changes only in the contents of the plot. Yet Verdi was a fertilising influence on the *verismo* school from Ponchielli to Puccini, and on modern Italian opera until Dallapiccola. *La Traviata* contains the seeds of a dramatic style which was as important for the future as the aesthetic theories of the *Ring*.

Brahms, who as a young composer had for a time been influenced by Wagner, inspired absolute music with new vitality in the chamber music, symphonies and concerti that he wrote after 1860. By accommodating into a new musical language old, almost forgotten chaconne and passacaglia forms, modal harmonies and baroque techniques of rhythm and phrase-structure, he set a pattern that remained viable in the music of the twentieth century. Reger, Hindemith, Busoni and Elgar profited from his example. 'Torniamo all'antico e sarà un progresso', as Verdi put it with the terse insight worthy of creative genius. Nor is his saying any less true through being constantly invoked by the enemies of genius.

The history of modern music is rich in instances of reversion and self-revision. When Strauss overstepped the limits of tonality in *Salome* and *Elektra*, he was overcome with apprehension at the enigmatic world of darkness he had opened up. He felt he could go no further with the boldness that had marked his work until that time (summer 1908). Torn as he was in his mind between the warring influences of Mozart and Wagner, he deliberately turned his back on the *neudeutsch* progressive ideology he had himself personified until that time. With *Der Rosenkavalier*, composed between May 1909 and September 1910, a traditional beauty and grace came back to modern music. Brilliant, prolonged tonal passages, which had been used only sporadically and for contrast in Jochanaan's scenes in *Salome* and the A flat music of *Elektra*, illuminate the entire *Rosenkavalier* score. Even the few interspersed moments of polytonality, such as the 'out of tune' celesta triads of the 'silver rose' music, do not dim the overall tonal brightness. Strauss ironically caps his anachronistic style by giving the waltz rhythm full rein. The action of the opera, of course, takes place before the waltz era, at the time of Maria Theresia. Strauss felt, however, that minuets and gavottes were not satisfactory means of illustrating a comedy of disguises and *mésalliances*. The very music assumes the garb of a later epoch, even if not that of the twentieth century in which it was written. When *Der Rosenkavalier* came to La Scala, Milan shortly after its premiere at Dresden, the Futurists protested at Strauss's 'betrayal' of modern music. In fact, however, *Der Rosenkavalier* does not cancel the achievements of *Salome* and *Elektra*. Indeed, it carries over techniques of harmony and orchestration used in the two earlier works and thereby, retroactively as it were, helps our understanding of them. In *Die Frau ohne Schatten*, composed between 1914 and 1918, Strauss found his way back once more to many of the radical formulae of *Salome* and *Elektra*. In the interim, though, he had made another creative volte-face. *Ariadne auf Naxos* (1911–12) saw a reduction of the gigantic orchestra of the earlier operas into a chamber ensemble of thirty-five players.

In 1906 Schoenberg undertook a similar retrenchment. The vast scores of *Pelleas und Melisande* (1903) and the Six Songs with Orchestra Op. 8 (1904) were succeeded by the Chamber Symphony for fifteen solo instruments. The possibilities of compositional technique and musical language which resulted were taken even further in *Pierrot Lunaire* with its ensemble of only eight instruments (five players). Stravinsky, too, having written *Le Sacre du printemps* (1912–3) for an outsize orchestra, then showed a preference for chamber ensembles with a small number of highly contrasting instruments, particularly in works until *L'Histoire du soldat* (1918). The score of *L'Histoire du soldat* looks like that of a skeleton symphony orchestra, with clarinet and bassoon for woodwind, cornet and trombone for brass, and violin and double-bass for strings. Along with these chamber ensembles a chamber-music style entered the language of modern music, which until then had mostly dealt in mammoth-sized orchestration. If there was a loss in orchestral lavishness and variety of tone-colour, there was a corresponding gain in the clarity of polyphonic argument. Not that the belief in continuous progress through the use of ever greater massings of instruments had vanished for good. In the Songs with Orchestra Op. 22 (1913–6) Schoenberg sought to create a new orchestral style by means of choric dispositions of instruments. The oratorio *Die Jakobsleiter*, begun in 1917 but never completed, was to have called for a gigantic orchestra of twenty oboes, twenty-four clarinets, twenty bassoons, twelve horns, ten trumpets, eight trombones, six double-bass tubas, eight harps, fifty violins, thirty violas, thirty cellos and double-basses and more besides, not to mention thirteen soloists and a choir of over seven hundred. However, knowing as we do the intellectual and spiritual assumptions that lay behind the oratorio, we can be sure that Schoenberg was not motivated by a positivist faith that progress would come with ever larger numbers. He visualised a highly variegated use of orchestral colour, and the choric treatment of individual timbres had a function to perform within this scheme. The chamber-music clarity of the texture of *Die Jakobsleiter* is quite different from the massive sonorities of a Straussian score, such as the *Alpensymphonie* that was also composed during the First World War. In his later works Schoenberg showed a preference for chamber-music ensembles.

But there were other instances of revision and reversion which had nothing to do with orchestral numbers. Opponents of modern music constantly reproached it for being complicated and unintelligible. Every art-form that breaks with received ideas of technique and structure meets with this reproach. The liquidation of tonality and the introduction of new asymmetrical metres had led to a crisis of comprehension even before the First World War. The two famous scandals provoked by performances of modern works in 1913 are significant. On 31 March, at a concert in the Grosse Musikvereinssaal in Vienna, the premiere of Berg's *Altenberg Lieder* broke up in a free fight and order had to be restored by the police. On 29 May the first performance of Stravinsky's *Le Sacre du printemps* under Pierre Monteux at the Théâtre des Champs-Élysées in Paris aroused a similar reaction. Today both works are in the standard repertoire; at that time the novelty of their musical language seemed provocative and outrageous.

The relationship between a work of art and its audience is the sum of complex aesthetic, psychological and social conditions. At all times a cleavage has separated the art designed for a wide audience from that which is for the connoisseur. In the latter, the degree of expertise may reach a level where the artist is able to conduct what amounts almost to a private conversation with an identifiable, well-informed audience. A partnership-situation of this kind actually existed in classical China, where the composer performed for a single listener who was fully conversant with the composer's ideas. Composers of the Ars Nova in France and Italy in the fourteenth century wrote for a very small circle of highly-cultured experts and patrons. Opera, too, originated in a similarly small circle of connoisseurs in Florence in about 1600. However, in both these periods music of a popular kind was also being produced, such as the songs which were being sung in villages or in the city streets. Some of these, such as *L'Homme armé*, were then taken over by the Netherlands contrapuntists and incorporated into highly complex sacred compositions using the full armoury of canonic and mirror techniques.

In the leading musical nations of Europe folk music has disappeared as a living, fertilising force. Folk songs and folk dances are, of course, still handed down and they are still kept alive in rural areas. But folk music has become the legacy of the past. The folk song handed down from one peasant generation to the next was supplanted in the course of the nineteenth century by the urban hit-song, usually supplied by stage productions. Parisian and Viennese operetta were a chief source of popular music of this kind and gave it wide currency. Young people in modern cities today sing popular hits and not the folk songs that have been driven from urban life. Since the twenties talking films have expanded the outlets of urban popular music, reinforced more recently by the powerful mass media of radio, television and the gramophone record.

Dwindling audiences for increasingly esoteric contemporary

music face young composers with an intellectual and economic problem. Comparisons between their own minimal circulation and the astronomical sales of light music gives them considerable food for thought. What can one say for a system which permits highly serious works to be heard only by a tiny group of experts? The issue was particularly acute for those German and Austrian composers who made the most radical innovations in musical language. One of the Viennese composers who endeavoured to find a solution in the middle twenties was Ernst Křenek (born 1900). In his *Selbstdarstellung* of 1948 Křenek described the tussle that took place between two of his chief preoccupations at that time: between esotericism on the one hand and his desire to make an impact on the public on the other. Having written harsh, dissonant music avoiding tonality that had made a considerable impression at avant-garde music festivals, he suddenly switched to the opposite extreme. His comic opera, *Der Sprung über den Schatten* was an uninhibited, cheeky rejection of the portentous profundities of his modernist contemporaries and of his own earlier compositions. The work takes in its sweep modish foxtrots, a parody of Offenbach in the form of a *galop*, characters from the cinema of the grotesque, a choir of masochists, and an orchestra with a banjo, motor-horn and a train whistle. At about the same time Křenek came into contact with contemporary French art and was immediately captivated by its lightness of touch.

I came to the conclusion that the assumptions underlying my work until that time were untenable. According to my new outlook, music should conform to the generally accepted needs of the community for which it was written; it should be useful, entertaining and practical.

It was with this conviction that Křenek wrote the libretto and music of his jazz opera *Jonny spielt auf* (1925–6). It was an enormous success when it was first produced in Leipzig in 1927 and during the next two years it was staged at over a hundred theatres throughout Europe. The work was even produced in Soviet Russia and the United States. It set the pattern for a whole series of similar works, which were generally lumped together as *Zeitopern*. They were all remarkable for their blend of popular music, highly up-to-date compositional techniques, new-fangled machinery and the depiction of fashionable hero-figures of current mythology.

Despite his unprecedented success, Křenek did not pursue this path any further. However, thanks to his dealings with these forms, his style acquired a lightness of touch which benefited his later, more serious compositions. His *Reisebuch aus den österreichischen Alpen* (1929) conspicuously reverts to romantic techniques; the work is a Schubert-like song-cycle whose words (by the composer himself) are a curious mixture of modern worldliness and lyrical-cum-philosophical speculation.

Křenek was a pupil of Franz Schreker (1878–1934), whose operas *Der ferne Klang* (1901–10 first performed 1912), *Die Gezeichneten* (1913–15, first performed 1918) and *Der Schatzgräber* (1915–18, first performed 1920) had a leading place on the German, and to some extent the non-German, stage in the golden years of opera in the twenties. Schreker's music is a distinctive blend of modern harmony that approaches the very frontiers of tonality, Italian *bel canto* in the style of Puccini, and a use of sonorities derived from French impressionism. He was an outstanding teacher, and as director of the Berlin Hochschule für Musik from 1920 to 1933 he trained a large number of pupils, who included among others Křenek and Alois Hába. He was also a life-long friend of Schoenberg.

Considerations such as led Křenek to popular music were fundamentally alien to the Schoenbergians. Only one of Schoenberg's pupils wrote music with a deliberate mass appeal: Hanns Eisler, who changed his musical aims in the middle twenties. Eisler had studied under Schoenberg in Vienna from 1918 to 1924 and during this time had written chamber music in an extended tonality and in twelve-note technique. He was already connected with socialist circles at that time. He wrote in an autobiographical note:

I moved to Berlin in about the autumn of 1924. Artur Schnabel showed an interest in my compositions and his pupils played my piano music. I earned my living as a composer and teacher but it was the workers' movement that

Hindemith (1895–1963) rehearsing Beethoven's Ninth Symphony at Bayreuth in 1953. He always wrote 'playable' music for the instruments on several of which he was himself a skilled performer. As an energetic teacher for many years in Germany and the United States he was influential, but his harmonic theory of chords and 'gradients' related to a root was naive and hardly a match for the rigour of Schoenbergian atonal theory.

attracted me. This led to a conflict with my teacher Arnold Schoenberg, who disapproved of such activities. At the time I was writing piano music, chamber music, vocal and orchestral works which were performed at the music festivals in Baden-Baden and Berlin. I had a certain amount of success; but I was dissatisfied. I didn't care for the conventional public. I wanted to say something new and for that I needed new listeners. So I had to begin again from the beginning.

We will have more to say later concerning Eisler's subsequent musical development, which was entirely determined by his political beliefs. His *Zeitungsausschnitte* (1926) for soprano and piano, with their caustic parodies of romantic lyricism, show him going over to a radically simplified style. Eisler's meeting with Bertolt Brecht had a decisive effect on his art.

Hindemith was another composer who sought to bring modern music to new classes of listeners. His vocal and instrumental compositions for amateurs and school-children, such as the *Spielmusik* and the Three-part Songs Op. 43, and the *Schulwerk* for string players Op. 44, were composed in 1927. They were followed by the *Sing-und Spielmusiken für Liebhaber und Musikfreunde* Op. 45, which include the often-performed *Frau Musica*, canons for two voices and instruments, and other pieces, all radically simplified in their musical language. In *Neues vom Tage* (1929) Hindemith followed Křenek's example by writing a comic *Zeitoper*. The music is full of parodies; the heroine Laura sings an aria in her bath in praise of the hot water supply. The plot centres round a divorce case; jazz rhythms are set against bold harmonies and polyphony. In Hindemith's case this reduced style was at first used playfully and without concern for fundamental aesthetic considerations. This tallied with his uncomplicated, 'practical' attitude towards composition: he worried little about aesthetic principles and remained wholly absorbed in the activity of music-making. His skill as a violinist and viola player, in theatre orchestras and in the then famous Amar string quartet, and the fact that he was at home with every instrument and every technique of composition, stood in practical contrast to the abstractionist, quasi-scientific theories of the Schoenberg school. This craftsman's attitude had an important bearing on the compositional techniques of modern music: it later prepared the ground for Hindemith's own more diversified, generalised process of revision.

Like Eisler, Hindemith was associated for a short while with Brecht, with whom he wrote the *Lehrstück* (1929), a work highly critical of society. His later development, however, led by way of old German folk song to a neo-baroque style that was somewhat analogous to the retrospective method of Stravinsky. Hindemith's growing seriousness and his leaning towards the past found powerful expression in the oratorio *Das Unaufhörliche* (1931), written in collaboration with Gottfried Benn. The work's impressive text affirms its opposition to materialism and the growing mechanisation of the modern world; Hindemith's music is polyphonic in inspiration and is based on broad, straightforward melodic writing. Soon after this philosophical work came the libretto and music for the opera *Mathis der Maler*, in which Hindemith uses the figure of the painter Grünewald to personify artistic genius in its stand against all political pressures.

Much of the music of *Mathis* is restorative in style. More room is given to extended tonal passages than ever before in Hindemith. The score makes considerable use of Gregorian chant and traditional religious folk songs. Twelve-note music is sometimes touched on in passing, but without far-reaching implications as to compositional technique. As in Hindemith's earlier stage works, notably *Cardillac* (1926), the structural framework is provided by classical and baroque vocal and instrumental forms.

From the first, Hindemith was anxious to draw up a theoretical foundation for his works. As a young composer under the influence of Schoenberg he had crossed the frontiers of tonality and had often favoured extravagant harmonic methods involving types of chord which had no place in traditional harmony. The more he incorporated traditional elements into his works, the more opposed he became to the idea of music without tonal ties. Driven into emigration by political events in Germany, he settled in the United States in 1940 and there continued the teaching career he had begun at the Berlin Hochschule für Musik in 1927. During his last years in Berlin, from 1934 to 1936, he wrote the theoretical part of a textbook on composition which was published in two parts in 1937 and 1939 under the title *Unterweisung im Tonsatz*.

In his book Hindemith starts from the natural harmonic series and derives the chromatic scale from the overtones. This enables him to relate the most outlying harmonic phenomena to a root. The procedure is somewhat contrived and is in parts highly speculative. Hindemith also uses his theory of roots to establish a kind of chordal hierarchy and introduces the fruitful notion of the '*harmonische Gefälle*' ('harmonic gradient'). In the analytical section of the book he applies his theory of chords to compositions ranging from the fourteenth century to the present day. He analyses a monophonic medieval piece, the *Dies Irae*, a ballade by Machaut, the Three-part Invention in F minor by Bach, Wagner's *Tristan* Prelude, the first movement of Stravinsky's Piano Sonata, Schoenberg's Piano Piece Op. 33a and his own Prelude to *Mathis der Maler*.

The Schoenberg is the most dubious of these analyses. It is reminiscent of attempts to interpret the shapes of natural objects by reading into them the features of Dante or the outlines of a leaping horse; the way in which the ancients grouped the stars into constellations which they named the Great Bear, the Lyre, or the Scorpion, had this same naivety. Hindemith did not stop at theory. He applied his conclusions to his earlier compositions. The harmonic writing of the earlier works had always been original and had frequently shown strokes of genius; the *Marienleben* song-cycle (1924) of poems by Rilke, the opera *Cardillac* and other works were now thoroughly revised, and chord-progressions which had no place in his theory were replaced by progressions based on the new 'harmonic gradient'.

No composer of the twenties and thirties made a more complete volte-face than Kurt Weill. Weill was born in Dessau in 1900, the same year as Křenek, and joined Busoni's master class in 1921. The works he wrote while serving his apprenticeship, however, notably the Concerto for violin and wind (1924), were little affected by Busoni's 'young classicism'. Weill was closer to Mahler and Schoenberg than to Latin formalism. His early operatic essays of the years 1925 to 1927 – *Der Protagonist, Der Zar lässt sich photographieren* (both with libretti by Georg Kaiser) and the ballet-opera *Royal Palace* (text by Iwan Goll) – were written in an expressionistic style with interpolations of jazz and tango rhythms.

At the Baden-Baden chamber music festival of 1929:
Weill, Hindemith, and Brecht are at left, centre and right.

121

In 1927 Weill met Bertolt Brecht, and was immediately won over
to his views on drama. They first collaborated in the spring of 1927
in the Songspiel *Mahagonny*, a concise work consisting of five poems
from Brecht's *Hauspostille*, some with melodies of Brecht's own.
The work was later expanded into the full-length opera, *Aufstieg
und Fall der Stadt Mahagonny* (1929). Between the two came *Die
Dreigroschenoper*. This work, as is well known, is a modern adapta-
tion of the *Beggar's Opera* by Gay and Pepusch, produced in
London in 1728. The songs are the chief feature of the opera, as
they were in *Mahagonny*, and are a deliberate rejection of the complexities of modern music. Melodies of the utmost simplicity are
linked with primitive tonal harmonies and simple dance rhythms.
Instead of modulating, the music simply jumps from one key to the
next. The vocal parts are straightforward enough to be performed
by actors, while the orchestra is a dance band with a few jazz

instruments. It is ideal music for the stage and its tunes can be whistled after a single hearing.

Weill went much further even than Křenek's jazz experiments. *Die Dreigroschenoper* was also a far greater success than any of the other *Zeitopern* of the twenties. Weill's skill emerges through all the primitive effects in the score. A light musician with an average musical training could never have written melodies of such simple yet sophisticated plasticity. This seems to be the secret of the work's lasting appeal. *Die Dreigroschenoper* has been performed the world over for forty years; the *Moritat* of Mack the Knife is an 'evergreen', a hit-song that seems to grow younger from one decade to the next. Weill and Brecht have remained a vital influence on the subsequent development of opera. Their *Song* genre has made its mark in the work of Eisler, Paul Dessau, Rudolf Wagner-Regeny and Boris Blacher, and in American musicals from the thirties onwards.

Those composers who believed that the only future for music lay in ever greater complexity were bound to regard *Die Dreigroschenoper* as a shocking, childish prank. Was it not a vulgar betrayal of the modern movement? Did it not frivolously abandon the ground that an earlier generation had won after such bitter struggle? Schoenberg and his followers were compelled to condemn the Brecht-Weill partnership, just as they had attacked Eisler's plunge into social criticism. 'Weill has given us back the *Dreivierteltakt*', said Schoenberg with bitter irony.

The more serious argument against such music was that it was cheap. Compared with involved twelve-note structures, it seemed all too easy to write. In point of fact, however, a simple style often poses greater problems than a complex one. A creative artist who submits to self-imposed rules and to rules inherent in his material is driven into a position of dependence which may be crippling. In many cases composers of little talent find it easier to comply with a system of rules, because of the opportunities for camouflage.

Rules of construction in art can be mastered in a purely technical way, but the result is pseudo-art owing nothing to inspiration. Romain Rolland, in his novel *Jean-Christophe*, portrays an artillery officer who can turn out highly complicated canons with great facility. The officer shows them proudly to Jean-Christophe, who finds to his astonishment that for all their ingenuity they are devoid of artistic value. The more music employs well-defined and easily-learned rules of construction, the greater the dangers of misuse. It may take considerable moral courage to dispense with a system of rules and the mere parade of complexity for its own sake.

Aesthetic and moral considerations both affect the artist's attitudes, but the two are not always compatible. There have always been situations when they have come into conflict. Insofar as art is a sublimation of the play instinct, it tends to become autonomous, and it is often the creative artists with the greatest talent who most indignantly repulse all attempts at interference by outsiders. The autonomy of art is determined by the extent to which the artist himself is independent of external institutions. But his independence is limited in ways that are not always merely institutional. Every creative artist subscribes to the general principles of a *Weltanschauung*, religion or political philosophy which he holds to be true. If his work comes into variance with these beliefs, some conflict is inevitable. The great world religions have used the arts in numerous ways for the purpose of capturing souls. Christianity has been the greatest source of artistic inspiration in the West for the last two thousand years. Yet as early as the Middle Ages the Church found it necessary to combat music's growing autonomy. The words of the sacred texts were becoming harder to follow; melismatic embellishments of single syllables were bringing about a dangerous predominance of music over text; the growth of polyphony was beginning to impair the music's original sacred purpose.

With the edicts of the Council of Trent in the middle of the sixteenth century, wide-ranging restrictions were imposed on the arts of polyphony. Even Palestrina, the greatest composer of sacred music in this period, thereafter lent his art to the new doctrine of simplicity. Musical considerations bowed before the power of the church; composers met the church's demands. The Palestrina reform, embodied in works such as the *Missa Papae Marcelli*, is the

124

classic example of a revision in music induced or imposed by external institutions. This is not to say that the argument that would seek to justify interventions in the arts by appeal to Palestrina is valid in a modern context of power. The reforms of the Council of Trent applied only to the strictly limited field of sacred music; secular music was left completely untouched. As in other periods of history, two kinds of music existed side by side at this time. Often one and the same composer wrote in both styles. This was true of Palestrina, Monteverdi and almost all the great composers whose principal employment was with the church, even until the time of J. S. Bach and the young Mozart.

Modern states, if they have any interest in regulating artistic matters at all, aim at total integration. This indeed is the common factor between communist and fascist political systems. Both attempt to control every form of artistic and intellectual expression. Both are consequently obliged to set up rules of artistic production and can tolerate no contraventions of them.

After the collapse of the Russian, German and Austrian monarchies in 1917 and 1918, there seemed for a time to be a united front between modern art and revolutionary politics. Leading writers, painters, composers and producers in Soviet Russia received official State backing and were keen to offer the State their services. Futurist painting and literature, constructivist theatre, atonal music and functional architecture dominated the Russian cultural scene until the middle twenties. The writers Blok and Mayakovsky, the sculptors Tatlin, Pevsner and Gabo, the painters Kandinsky, Malevich and Lissitzky had a considerable impact on the younger Russian generation until 1922. Russian composers in the same period were influenced partly by the metaphysics of Scriabin and partly by Stravinsky and Prokofiev. The year 1924 saw the inauguration of the 'Evenings of New Western Music' in Leningrad, and the Moscow 'Association for Contemporary Music' also promoted modern works. The most important compositions of Hindemith, Křenek, Milhaud, Stravinsky and Schoenberg were performed at the Leningrad Philharmonic Hall. Soviet opera houses gave performances of *Wozzeck*, *Jonny spielt auf* and Schreker's *Der ferne Klang*.

It was in this avant-garde atmosphere that Dmitri Shostakovich (born 1906) grew up. He graduated from the Leningrad Academy of Music and soon attracted attention as a pianist and composer. His rich, many-sided musical personality came under the influence of modern Western music, particularly Stravinsky and Berg. The first performance of his First Symphony under Nicolai Malko in Leningrad in 1926 paved the way to his international renown. At this time, too, Soviet music critics were unanimous in their praise of the twenty-year old composer. Later they had reservations. Even Shostakovich's biographer and advocate, Ivan Martynov, wrote in his book on the composer in 1942:

> The music of the First Symphony reveals some features which were later to be points of departure for several creative errors on Shostakovich's part. Constructivism became an abstract-formalist end in itself; the grotesqueries merely grew into malevolent raillery; expressiveness was taken to the furthest extremes of intensity. Furthermore, his great facility carried with it a serious danger of laxity and superficiality, which was to come to the fore in certain works. Many years later this frivolity was reflected in the Mozartian clarities of the Sixth Symphony.

The same year, 1926, saw the birth of the slogan 'Social Realism', which was to play such an important part in the Stalin era.

In the meantime Shostakovich, besides writing orchestral and chamber works and the highly modernistic, difficult Piano Sonata, completed his first opera: *The Nose*, with a libretto based on the famous short story by Gogol. The work was composed between 1927 and 1928. The score demonstrates his astonishing resourcefulness in finding new and provocative means of expression. The vocal parts are mostly in recitative form and are highly burlesque in character. Shostakovich actually asks the singer of the part of the Nose to sing while holding his nose. The orchestra is used in a chamber-music fashion, and there are various imitations of natural noises, such as the tramping of horses, belches and so forth. There is a janitors' octet in which eight different newspaper advertisements

Shostakovich (b. 1906),
unassailably established as the
greatest Soviet composer of today.

are sung simultaneously. The interlude leading to the second scene is scored for percussion alone. In his critical account of the work Martynov draws analogies between it and non-representational painting and the 'box-like' architecture of the twenties. He also maintains that there were comparisons between the 1930 production at the Maly Opera House in Leningrad and the constructivist theatre of Meyerhold. The provocative sarcasm of the work found few admirers in Russia. After writing two ballet scores, *The Golden Age* (1930) and *The Bolt* (1931), and a considerable quantity of music for the theatre and films, Shostakovich composed the four-act opera *Lady Macbeth of Mtsensk*, later called *Katerina Ismailova*. The work was written between 1930 and 1932 and it was given its premiere at the Maly Opera House in Leningrad in 1934. Its libretto was based on a short story by Nicolai Leskov. The fate of the opera is well known. It was received with acclamation in Leningrad and was enthusiastically taken up abroad, in New York, Cleveland, London, Prague, Zürich, Stockholm and elsewhere. Then on 26 January 1936 an article appeared in the Moscow edition of *Pravda* denouncing the work crushingly and completely. The author of the article accused Shostakovich of deliberately standing music on its head and robbing it of any kinship with simple musical language. The work, he said, was based on a principle of negation, which in art implied a rejection of simplicity, realism, clarity of conception and a straightforward use of words.

The ugly distortions of the opera spring from the same source as similar distortions in painting, poetry, education and science.

Shortly after this attack *Lady Macbeth of Mtsensk* vanished from the Leningrad stage and from the Nemirovich-Danchenko Theatre in Moscow where a particularly well-prepared production had just got under way.

Shostakovich took these threatening criticisms to heart. He answered the official party censure by writing the Fifth Symphony (1937), whose autobiographical programme is entitled 'The growth of a personality'. His biographer Martynov says of the work:

He had been put through the test and now he told the story of himself and his experiences. . . . Shostakovich's personal fate coincided with that of countless human beings, and his listeners could not remain unmoved by such a faithful depiction of what they had themselves experienced.

Avowals of guilt and repentance are a feature of the Russian character. We are familiar with the great self-indictments in the plays of Ostrovsky and the novels of Tolstoy and Dostoievsky. They have the function of a public version of the religious confession of sin and their usefulness in unburdening the man who makes them should not be underestimated. It undoubtedly takes courage to make a confession of guilt of this kind. However, this task is made much easier in totalitarian states, inasmuch as the confession has to conform to political requirements. It then becomes difficult to say how far the self-accusation is genuine and how far it has been extracted under pressure.

Since 1937 Shostakovich has for the most part abandoned the modernistic experimentation that had been such an interesting and provocative feature of his early work. He has returned to tonality and romantic melody. He has composed slow movements filled with emotional tension. His tragic and triumphant march rhythms tell the story of the birth of a new socialist society. Only in the scherzi of his symphonies do we find the old sarcasm and banter. Now and then, as in the Ninth Symphony (1945), the mocking voice of the young experimentalist and admirer of Stravinsky can still be heard. On the whole, however, Shostakovich has adopted a romantic stance which derives particularly from Tchaikovsky and Mahler. He has acknowledged the 'sins' of his youth with Dostoievskian ruthlessness, promising not to repeat them. A readjustment of this order would have destroyed a lesser artistic personality. Shostakovich's outstanding imagination and ability as a symphonist and composer of chamber music have protected him from the fate that befell many minor Soviet composers.

Serge Prokofiev left Russia legally in 1918. He returned on a visit as a successful composer in 1927 and finally settled in his native

The police scene from *Katerina Ismailova* (in the London production). Shostakovich's opera was first produced in 1934; Stalin's personal disgust for its music was formally confirmed by *Pravda* in January 1936.

Prokofiev (1891–1953), already a brilliant innovator in Russia's musical life before the First World War, left the country in 1918. He returned nine years later on a visit, finally settling in the Soviet Union in the thirties as a successful composer to write among other music his ballet *Romeo and Juliet* and the Fifth Symphony.

country in 1934, only to meet with opposition in the same way as Shostakovich. In January 1948 Soviet composers, musicologists, singers, conductors, teachers and critics were invited to a conference of the Central Committee of the Communist Party in Moscow. A. Zhdanov on behalf of the Central Committee attacked several composers and certain members of the Union of Soviet Composers who were blocking the road to socialism, citing particularly Shostakovich and Prokofiev. He condemned 'formalism' and all departures from classical tradition and Russian popular idiom.

This [formalistic] tendency replaces natural, beautiful human music by music that is adulterated, vulgar and often downright pathological. . . . The Russian people assesses a a piece of music by the extent to which it reflects the spirit of the times and can be comprehended by the masses.

As early as February 1948 Prokofiev published a confession of guilt, though in it he also attempted to defend himself:

I have undoubtedly been guilty of atonality, though I am bound to say that from early on there were signs of an aspiration towards tonality in my works, once I recognised that the tonal structure of a work is comparable to a building constructed on a solid foundation, whereas an atonal structure is built on sand. . . . In some of my more recent works there are isolated moments of atonality. Without feeling any particular sympathy for them, I used them as a means of obtaining large-scale contrasts and of giving greater prominence to the tonal passages.

Elsewhere in the declaration he says:

I have not been . . . completely guiltless of formalist errors in my works, under the influence of certain Western trends.

He closes by announcing a new opera, *The Story of a Real Man*, and by promising that he 'will search for a clear musical language that can be understood and cherished by my people'.

The *autodafé* of the Spanish Inquisition was a solemn execution of judgment accompanied by confessions of guilt and vows of contrition. Time and again in the history of modern art there have been instances of revisions and reversions which have contained explicit confessions of this kind. For example, Stravinsky with every change of style has proclaimed his opposition to the aesthetic assumptions of his previous style. As a neo-classicist he had nothing but scorn and contempt for the folk-philosophy that had inspired his earlier music in so many ways. Later, as a repentant supporter of Schoenberg, he thundered no less scornfully against classicism, just as Schoenberg had done against Stravinsky's own neo-classical style in 1925. After 1940, the distinguished painter Chirico, whose work had been an important contribution to sur-realism, rejected everything that had made him famous when young and switched to a realistic neo-Renaissance manner. In the same way, Johannes R. Becher, one of the most revolutionary poets of German expressionism, burnt everything he had previously idolised. It was he who formulated the often quoted epigram: 'The hardest thing has been to achieve simplicity'. It might have been the motto of the music of Eisler.

7 The music of commitment

At all times musicians and non-musicians have disputed whether music has an autonomous existence of its own. One side has argued that music lives its own life as a formal world governed solely by its own laws. The other maintains, with good reason, that music necessarily serves a higher, or at least extra-musical, end. The same problem exists with other art-forms, of course, but they are object-bound in that they have links with objects and ideas lying outside themselves. Music is fundamentally non-representational. True, it can touch on the realms of physical objects or ideas, but only in a very few cases can it hold up a mirror to them. Musical forms have almost no parallels in the physical world. Natural phenomena may provide an occasional stimulus – echoes suggesting canons, bird-song suggesting vocal melisma – but that is all.

The romantics' attitude in this matter was ambivalent. During the romantic period the notion of *l'art pour l'art* had considerable currency – the notion that art should have no other aim than a sophisticated self-sufficiency. At the same time, however, there was a blurring of the frontiers between the different arts and a trend, as far as music was concerned, towards descriptiveness and 'symphonic poetry'. A composer like Chopin wrote and played for a small circle of connoisseurs, yet many of his compositions clearly expressed the Polish national feelings that animated him. Wagner took romantic harmony to extremes of chromatic refinement, particularly in *Tristan*, but he no more wanted music to be an isolated art-form than he did painting, literature, ballet or drama. His vision of the *Gesamtkunstwerk* went right against the doctrine of *l'art pour l'art*.

Music cannot expound beliefs. It can, however, reinforce the expression of a belief and make it more emphatic and persuasive. This should be remembered in any discussion of the use of music with texts whose authors seek to change the world. The desire to change mankind, the world, or preferably both, has always been the aim of founders of religions and of their modern counterparts, politicians and social theorists. Such men have always been aware that music can be as effective as the spoken or written word.

Yet words have a content or meaning that is basically capable of clear definition; music has no comparable meaning or sense. If it has a semantic content that can be clearly pinpointed, this is by virtue of definite conventions imposed on its own forms and formulae. When Plato, in the dialogue between Socrates and Glaucon, meticulously classified the musical modes into the melancholic (from which men and women should be protected), the intoxicating (which the guardians of the states should view with mistrust), and those encouraging the military virtues, he really had in mind the Mixolydian, Lydian, Dorian and Phrygian scales that were current in Athens for a period and had a quite specific significance. When in the twelfth century the church condemned the Ionian mode (our later C major) as the *modus lascivus*, it was referring to all the erotic songs that were using and vulgarising the Ionian mode at that time.

At one point in *Wozzeck* Berg uses the C major triad, the most well-thumbed chord of all, to depict the prosaic act of counting money. But apart from certain basic emotional effects, such as the use of 'natural' intervals (the octave, fifth and fourth) or march rhythms, music has no universalised semantics. It is not independent of the epoch or cultural context from which it springs. The politically committed humanist Settembrini in Thomas Mann's *Magic Mountain* confesses to his young German friends that he has a 'political aversion' to music, and Mann, with his deep love of music and in particular that of Wagner, knew why.

No religion has used music more fully or to greater effect than Christianity. For centuries in the West sacred subjects were the only ones deemed worthy and fitting of music. Countless forms, from Jewish antiphonal psalmody to the canon symbolic of the Imitation of Christ, originated in sacred music or came to acquire a sacred interpretation. The church itself has written one of the most significant chapters in the history of European music.

But music has also been used in the service of secular ideals. Could the philosophical musical works that followed in the wake of Enlightenment match earlier religious music in richness and tature? The question was first posed by the finale of Beethoven's Ninth Symphony, where Schiller's humanistic beliefs were grafted onto a symphonic form. The work did not set a pattern immediately to be followed, but in the longer run it influenced Wagner's music-dramas and the vocal symphonies of Mahler, which latter in their turn provided a link with the symphonies of Shostakovich.

After the First World War activist political movements in central Europe sought to use the arts to further their political aims. The left-wing Arbeiter-Sängerbund in Berlin attracted various composers, including Hans Tiessen and Stefan Wolpe. Progressive producers and dramatists like Piscator and Brecht found collaborators in Weill, Eisler and other composers. Hindemith was also associated with the left for a time.

One of the most striking facts about this period was that the middle-class centre was no better equipped to keep pace with these developments than was the extreme right. Political and social commitment lay to the left. Polyhymnia and Thalia followed the red flag.

Inspired by Brecht, Weill set the tone for left-wing music in the Weimar Reublic with his highly simplified, aggressive melodies and rhythms. The *Berliner Requiem*, the operas and the didactic pieces *Der Lindberg-Flug* and *Der Ja-Sager*, signalled a return in compositional terms to tonality and simple metres. Nonetheless, the Brecht-Weill political pieces were part and parcel of the bourgeois musical scene. *Die Dreigroschenoper* and *Mahagonny* figured in the repertoires of stage and civic theatres.

The showdown came in 1930, when a disagreement arose between the artistic directors of the festival Neue Musik Berlin and some of the authors of works that were to be performed. The directors were Hindemith, Heinrich Burkhard and George Schünemann. They had arranged for a didactic piece with Brecht and Eisler, but because of the political risks involved they asked to see the text before announcing the programme. Brecht and Eisler refused, in an open letter in which they called for the directors' resignations, claiming that 'they would do more good by protesting against attempts to censor modern music than by holding a music festival in the summer of 1930'. The festival went ahead. There were electronic compositions, original pieces for gramophone records, didactic works and children's operas; the composers included Ernst Toch, Hermann Reutter, Paul Dessau, Paul Höffer and Hindemith. The Brecht-Eisler didactic piece was not performed. Nor was Weill's *Ja-Sager* which he had withdrawn but which was being performed elsewhere.

The piece that was the cause of all this conflict was first performed in Berlin in December 1930. It was the oratorio *Die Massnahme* by Brecht, Eisler and the film producer Slatan Dudow. The performance was held late at night in the Berlin Philharmonic Hall before an audience of leading personalities from Berlin's theatrical, musical and literary life. The work was conducted by Karl Rankl, a former pupil of Schoenberg, who was at that time a conductor at Klemperer's Kroll opera. A workers' choir, an opera singer, and the actors Ernst Busch, Alexander Granach and Helene Weigel also took part.

Eisler's score is important as being the first large-scale work of politically committed music. It is written for a mixed choir (mostly in two parts) and an orchestra of brass and percussion. The piano is used as a symbol of bourgeois culture. The musical language exactly fulfils the work's didactic purpose, as for example at the point where Lenin's dictum: 'The clever man is not the one who makes no mistakes, but the one who quickly repairs them' is chanted in canon by the choir *a cappella*. Eisler was from then on the acknowledged master of communist music. He emigrated to Prague and then to Hollywood, returning to Vienna in 1949. He lived in East Berlin from 1950 until his death in 1962.

Not all members of the German avant-garde went over to communism in the thirties. Hindemith, although he was aware of the threat that fascism posed to the arts, adopted a conservative position, and his oratorio *Das Unaufhörliche* was the only major work that could stand comparison with the politically inflammatory music of Eisler and Weill. Gottfried Benn's text is a statement of the transitoriness of all human achievement, and it stands in the same relation to Brecht's activism as Hindemith's polyphony does to the simplified language of *Politmusik*.

During the Hitler period none of the attempts to create a national-socialist brand of music produced anything worthy of mention. Nor were any works of lasting quality produced in fascist Italy. A few non-conformist composers in the Hitler Youth were actually followers of Hindemith and Stravinsky, but none of them succeeded in achieving a distinctive style or in gaining much response from the public. The émigré composers, on the other hand, kept alive the central European belief that music might change the world.

These composers mostly found support in England and the United States, and to a lesser extent in Czechoslovakia and the Soviet Union. In 1939, for example, shortly before Hitler's invasion of Poland and a few days before the Warsaw Festival of the ISCM (banned by the Nazis), a three-day event of special cultural and political importance was held in London. It was called a 'Festival of Music for the People' and opened on 1 April with a parade of five hundred singers, a hundred dancers and a brass band. The festival's motto was 'Peace, Freedom and Work'. Works were contributed by Alan Bush, Norman Demuth, Elizabeth Lutyens, Alan Rawsthorne and Ralph Vaughan Williams. The programmes also contained political cantatas by Eisler, Schoenberg's 1907 chorus *Friede auf Erden*, and a work by the twenty-five year old Benjamin Britten, then still unknown. This work, *Ballad of Heroes*, with a text by W. H. Auden and Randall Swingler, commemorates the British members of the International Brigade who were killed in the Spanish Civil War. Britten has subsequently dealt mostly with very different themes, though they have still often been humanists and libertarian in character. The most important of his later works of this kind is the *War Requiem*, written for the re-dedication of Coventry Cathedral which was destroyed in Nazi air raids during the war. Alan Bush, on the other hand, has become the most out-and-out exponent of left-wing *Politmusik* in England. His operas *Wat Tyler* (1953), based on the Peasants' Revolt, and

Men of Blackmoor (1956) were first performed in East Germany, in Leipzig and Weimar respectively.

In 1938 a member of the German Embassy in Paris was shot dead by a young Jewish refugee. Michael Tippett, who until then had been known only for a double concerto and his chamber music, made this event the subject of an oratorio, *A Child of Our Time*, which caused a considerable stir when it was first performed in London in 1944. Even today it preserves its impact as a humane anti-fascist document of the highest artistic order.

The Russo-German composer Wladimir Vogel, a pupil of Busoni's in Berlin in the twenties, left Germany in 1933 and after a number of years of wandering settled permanently in Switzerland. While a refugee he composed the two parts of his gigantic oratorio *Thyl Claes* (1938–42) and 1943–5), based on *Thyl Ulenspiegel* by Charles de Coster. The work calls for soprano, two *Sprechstimmen*, speech-choir and large orchestra. It is a statement of conviction and a protest against tyranny and dictatorship. The first part deals with the fate of individuals, the second with the fate of the community as a whole. It was first performed under Ernest Ansermet in Geneva. Various technical devices are used for symbolic effect, such as the Love Chaconne which in inversion is changed vividly into a Song of Hate against Philip II. Vogel adds important new functions to the *Sprechstimme* over and beyond those achieved by Schoenberg.

Like German writers, American writers became involved in political problems and activities after the First World War. The demands that Dreiser, Upton Sinclair and to a lesser extent Sinclair Lewis made for a better society were echoed in the next generation by composers such as Marc Blitzstein. Blitzstein's socialist operas, the chief of which are *The Cradle will Rock* (1930) and *No for an Answer* (1941), have influenced the modern musical, particularly Bernstein's *West Side Story*. Weill, too, wrote for the American stage after settling in the United States, though Brecht's collaboration was something he could ill afford to lose.

During the Second World War American intellectuals became increasingly interested in the ideology and culture of their Soviet

Britten (b. 1913), to whose achievement
(he has written seven operas) and
encouragement the rebirth of English opera
after 1945 is almost entirely due.

allies. This led some composers to a certain measure of political commitment. Aaron Copland, George Antheil and others dedicated works to the Red Army – at the price of painful interrogations during the McCarthy era. In the Soviet Union there were naturally countless anti-fascist compositions following the line laid down in the thirties. Most of them have remained unknown outside Russia, or in the West at any rate. Who has heard a performance of Prokofiev's *1941 Suite* or his *Toast to Stalin*, for example, or of Shostakovich's *Oath to the People's Commissar?* The more or less concealed programmes of some of Shostakovich's symphonies also fall into the committed category.

Schoenberg was for a long period a convinced opponent of all art with a political content, particularly until 1933. This led to a serious breach with his pupil Eisler. Schoenberg often said that he did not want to become involved in political issues and that politics was for politicians, just as making shoes was for shoe-makers. Later, too, he had equally little time for 'artists who really and truly should have something better to say' and who 'meddle with theories of human betterment, although we all know from history where that leads to' – thus in a letter to Josef Rufer of 18 December 1947.

However, Schoenberg's very existence was put in jeopardy by the racial theories of National Socialism. Several years before, during the First World War, his view of life had begun to change and he had become increasingly occupied with religious questions. This was reflected in the oratorio *Die Jakobsleiter*, composed to his own text, the Zionist play *Der biblische Weg* (1925) and the unfinished opera Moses und Aron (1930–2), again composed to his own text. His retort to Hitler's armed challenge to humanity took the form of a setting of Byron's *Ode to Napoleon Bonaparte*. There could be little doubt, in the year 1944, against whom this masterly song of hatred was directed. And *A Survivor from Warsaw* (1948) reflected equally artistically and even more powerfully his horror at the inhumanity that could send millions of human beings to the gas chambers. During his years in America Schoenberg also wrote various articles on Jewish questions. At the request of an American

Jewish community he composed a setting of the traditional prayer *Kol Nidre* that is an important contribution to Jewish liturgy. The last works he wrote before his death in 1951 were the *Modern Psalms*, the third of which, for speaker, four-part mixed chorus and orchestra, he was able only partly to complete.

After the war, composers from those countries where fascism had first arisen left it to writers to come to terms with the past. They themselves threw off the strait-jacket into which they had been thrust. After twelve years of enforced piety to tonality they were now able to write atonally, and they proceeded to expand Schoenberg's note-row method into a serial language. Even serial composers with left-wing views, such as Pierre Boulez, remained aloof from a music of commitment.

Louis Durey (born 1888), a French composer of the older generation who had earlier been recruited by Cocteau into the 'Six' group, later became converted to communism. His *Grève de la faim* is one of the most important French post-war works of political *engagement*. So too are the works of Serge Nigg, a much younger dodecaphonic composer (*Le Fusillié inconnu*, 1949, and *Chant des mineurs*, 1952).

In the Soviet-orientated German Democratic Republic the arts, particularly drama and music, are predominantly political in character. Brecht settled in East Berlin after the war, and in Eisler and Dessau, who had also returned from America, he found two composers who shared his views. His collaboration with Dessau resulted in the music and songs for *Mother Courage*, *The Good Woman of Szechuan* and *The Caucasian Chalk Circle*, and the opera *The Trial of Lucullus*, which for political reasons had to be altered after its dress rehearsal and renamed *The Condemnation of Lucullus* (1951). Dessau completed an opera based on the play *Herr Puntila und sein Knecht* only after Brecht's death. In the melodrama *Lilo Herrmann* (text by Friedrich Wolf) he described the fate of a socialist chemistry student murdered by the Nazis.

While in America Eisler, apart from composing film music, had written a series of cantatas to words by Brecht which were later put together in his *Deutsche Sinfonie*. The work was first performed under Walter Goehr in 1959 at the State Opera in East Berlin. His Lenin cantata, a requiem with words by Brecht, was also written in America. During his years in East Berlin Eisler wrote numerous choruses and cantatas, as well as the collection of *Neue deutsche Volkslieder*, which are settings of poems by the former expressionist poet Becher, who had returned from the Soviet Union.

In countries where the arts are an organ of the one-party state creative artists are given every facility for producing works of political commitment. These works, however, are not the professions of belief of a solitary individual in the midst of a hostile world. They are conformist and entail no risk. They are a part of the artist's obligations.

To proclaim support for communism within bourgeois society is quite a different matter. True, the artist in this case enjoys the privilege of free speech. But if he exercises the privilege, he is setting himself up against official political opinion. He risks the danger that threatens any opposition group: isolation and private and professional ostracism.

If England led the way in left-wing vocal music in the thirties, Italy has increasingly come to the fore since 1945. Most of the works of Luigi Dallapiccola centre round the notion of liberty. His *Canti di prigionia*, the opera *Il prigioniero* and many later works are defences of freedom against inhumanity and dictatorship. They are at once an outward protest and the expression of an inner need to come to terms with the past: Italian fascism and the Nazi occupation are fought on the battleground of the emotions. The works can thus be seen as an indictment of all forms of totalitarian suppression. This is not a party-political form of commitment but a siding with humanity against the use of force. The message of the numerous compositions that have been written denouncing the terrible mass-murder of Hiroshima can be generalised in a similar way. Luigi Nono on the other hand has increasingly made his vocal compositions expressions of socialist beliefs: notably *La Victoire de Guernica* (1954) with words by Paul Eluard; *Il canto sospeso* (1956),

Dallapiccola (b. 1904) is the first Italian composer to have adopted Schoenberg's and Berg's ideas and to have made them part of his own musical language. He writes mainly for voices, including operas and pieces for voice and orchestra; also for piano, an instrument on which he is a brilliant performer.

which is based on last letters by resistance fighters; and the opera *Intolleranza* (1960), which has been performed in Cologne and Boston. Nono, however, has found himself somewhat between two camps: although his works are communist in outlook, he employs techniques that have been most vehemently condemned in official communist pronouncements on music. In particular, he uses the controversial technique in his vocal writing of breaking up the text into syllables and even letters which are to be sung separately, even though this may lead to total incomprehensibility. The result is artistically interesting, but the subject-matter, on which a politically committed artist should surely place greater value, loses all its impact.

To fall between two stools in this way has been seen to happen often enough in recent art. Until 1952 a composer in the communist world who espoused twelve-note composition or electronic and pointillistic distortions of his texts was putting his creative life in the balance. Even today to do so means to be deprived of state support, publication and public performance, particularly in the Soviet Union and the GDR. Nono's music for

Weiss's political stage work *Ermittlung* is based on 'compositional techniques which are available only in an electronic studio'. It uses a children's choir, solo soprano, chorus, instruments and sounds that are produced electronically. Quite deliberately no doubt, Nono has thus dissociated himself from the Weill-Eisler brand of simplified didactic music for the masses. This syncretistic approach, using very recent, even experimental compositional techniques, is characteristic of the new music of commitment. The Milanese composer Giacomo Manzoni, for example, in his anti-fascist opera *Atomic Death*, combines jazz and baroque sonorities with the most up-to-date technical means.

Music can only give further emphasis to words. Rouget de Lisle's *Marseillaise* preserves its revolutionary élan to the present day because history has endowed its melody with such lasting significance. The *music* of the *Marseillaise* cannot serve as a model for politically committed composition; nor can the songs of Weill and Eisler or Nono's syntheses.

Any political music can be taken up by the other side by a simple exchange of texts. Musicians themselves may be politically committed, certainly – but their works must be judged in accordance with aesthetic, not political, criteria.

The same is true of religious music. The nineteenth century saw the disappearance of the composer owing his living principally to the church. By 1800 most composers of importance had followed in the footsteps of Mozart and Beethoven and become free creative artists, a position that was strengthened in the course of the nineteenth century by the development of copyright law. If a composer chose to make a setting of a sacred text, as Verdi and Rossini did from time to time, that was his private affair. He was no longer supported by commissions from the church. He might compose a number of religious works, but they would be on the same footing as his secular works. Bruckner wrote several Masses and other sacred pieces in addition to his nine symphonies, although he was no longer in the church's employ after he had moved to Vienna.

Various major twentieth-century composers have written no

sacred or liturgical music at all. There is none in Strauss, Debussy or Ravel. Religious subjects are found in some of Mahler's symphonies, in the Second (the 'Resurrection') and the Eighth, where the traditional hymn *Veni Creator Spiritus* is used together with an excerpt from *Faust*. Only Max Reger, with his organist's background, devoted any major part of his work to liturgical subjects.

In the New Music the picture is different. Webern, Schoenberg's pupil of longest standing, followed his teacher's example until the First World War and wrote 'pure' vocal and instrumental music without philosophical or religious connections. But after military service between 1915 and 1916 had exposed him to a war whose horrors he had already clearly foreseen, he became gradually converted to a deeper religious faith.

In 1915 Webern made his first setting of a religious text, one of the numerous pious folk songs by anonymous authors or from *Des Knaben Wunderhorn* for which he had a particular affection. The song is the first in the Op.12 collection:

> Der Tag ist vergangen, die Nacht ist schon hier,
> Gute Nacht, o Maria, bleib ewig bei mir.

Complex chordal relationships are accommodated within a simple homophonic accompaniment; the taboo on note-repetitions produces a dense twelve-note exposition that gives way to free panchromaticism. In 1917 the fifth of the Sacred Songs Op. 15 was written. The words: 'Fahr' hin, o Seel, zu deinem Gott, der dich aus nichts gestaltet', are naive in their piety, rather like the wayside crosses that Webern used to see every day in his childhood in Carinthia. He treats it in the canonic style he had learned from Heinrich Isaac and Schoenberg.

These religious songs give Webern a place within the religious movement that overtook German expressionism in the years following 1918. The same tide of feeling gave rise to the religious, visionary works of painters and sculptors such as Nolde, Schmidt-Rottluff, Rouault and Barlach. Webern's whole creative effort takes the form of submission to self-imposed constraints: the

effort finds its particular fulfilment in the use of canon, notably in the settings of Latin Passion texts Op. 16, where, as in medieval theory, canonic imitation is used to symbolise the Imitation of Christ. The canons are in two and three parts, for clarinet, bass clarinet and high soprano; their mirror forms are a gem of Netherlands-style polyphonic technique. They were his last work in a 'free-atonal' chromatic style. In his next work, the three sacred Folk Texts of 1924, he adopted Schoenberg's method of composition with twelve notes. Webern, who always took the Bible and *Faust* with him when he travelled, composed further religious works after becoming acquainted with the mystical poetry of Hildegard Jone. The Songs Op. 25, the choral work *Das Augenlicht* and the two Cantatas, all with words by Hildegard Jone, are written in a highly introverted, reduced language using new and rarified combinations of notes.

Igor Stravinsky, a devout Catholic in private life, did not write the first of his many religious compositions until 1926, a *Pater Noster* for mixed *a cappella* choir. The *Symphony of Psalms* of 1930, based on psalms from the Vulgate, was 'composed to the glory of God [and] dedicated to the Boston Symphony Orchestra on its fiftieth anniversary'. The second movement, a double fugue, is a monumental specimen of modern dissonant counterpoint. Two small unaccompanied choruses, a *Credo* and an *Ave Maria*, followed soon after.

The *Mass* for mixed choir and double wind quintet of 1947 signalled a complete change in Stravinsky's musical thinking. The work's retrospective polyphony at one and the same time harks back to medieval models and shows his first use of small note-series, though these are not yet dodecaphonic. In the *Canticum Sacrum* (1956), *Threni* (1958) and various smaller works, Stravinsky has followed his new mentors, Schoenberg and Webern, and used twelve-note techniques in structures of varying degrees of strictness. In one of his conversations with Robert Craft, Stravinsky has said:

Webern is for me the *juste de la musique* and I do not hesitate to shelter myself by the beneficent protection of his not yet canonized art.

The year 1936 saw a modification of the anti-romantic stance that had governed French music since 1918. A group of composers came into prominence calling themselves 'La Jeune France': Yves Baudrier, André Jolivet, Daniel Lesur and Olivier Messiaen, whose name was already being noted. They dissociated themselves from the anti-romanticism of the followers of Satie and advocated goals that may be termed romantic and religious.

Of the four, Messiaen was the most closely bound to the Christian liturgical tradition. As organist of La Trinité in Paris his chief occupation has been in the service of God. As early as 1931 he wrote an introduction to his work *Offrandes oubliées* in which he declared his adhence to the Catholic faith. The *Quatuor pour la fin du temps*, written in a German prisoner-of-war camp, also has a commentary of a mystical, theological nature. His religious commitment also emerges explicitly in his numerous organ pieces, most of which have sacred titles, and in his piano works, including the *Visions de l'Amen* for two pianos (1943) and *Vingt regards sur l'enfant Jesus* (1944). Messiaen has always explored new ground in compositional technique, and since 1945 he has been a major influence. His religious faith has not stood in the way of his humanity and universality: he has great insight into the music of India and the Indians of Latin America, and a passionate interest in the bird-song of countries all over the world. Such disparate elements of style could be unified only by a creative talent of considerable independence and bold imagination. Messiaen is the most versatile and interesting of the committed composers of the twentieth century.

Webern and Messiaen have had great influence on the development of recent music, particularly in Germany and France. Both are personifications of the committed composer who has remained a considerable artist. Webern, in fact, who is reputed to have said his prayers every night with a simple childish piety, often on his knees, was at the same time a convinced socialist. He conducted workers' choirs for many years and from 1922 until 1934 he conducted the Workers' Symphony Concerts in Vienna. Christianity and socialism were the corner-stones of his intellectual and spiritual make-up. True, he never wrote music dealing with political ideas as for example Brecht or his friend Eisler did. But the strictness with which he held to his philosophy of life conditioned the nature of his music. Its canons and variations of small motivic cells constitute a wholly new language.

Messiaen is too imbued with a religious attitude to life to find room for political or social beliefs. But his complex interlocking musical structures likewise reflect his mind's attachment to theology and to universalist syntheses.

8 Folk-music and exotic music

We can understand the art of an epoch only if we recognise that it necessarily has several different planes of significance. It may be hard for a creative artist to recognise that other men's ideas can be as inspired and vital as his own. He often tends to condemn what is merely a product of different artistic preconceptions. The recurrent complaint that there is a gulf between the art which is for the initiated and that which appeals to the naive general public, cannot be answered.

But have things ever been otherwise? In the Middle Ages there was one art for the experts and another for the lay public: an irreconcilable, or apparently irreconcilable, split between the riddle canon and the isorhythmic motet on the one hand, the *Minnesang* and dancing songs on the other.

Looking at the history of the arts in broad terms, at the ebb and flow of their outward forms, two tendencies, at times in conflict and at times reconciled, may always be seen. One is born of a feeling of community and a desire to be understood. The other stems from a feeling of individuality, with creative man seen as the measure of all things. Now it is certainly the creative individual who makes discoveries and brings about the enrichments of language that are the medium of all Western intellectual and artistic development. But equally certainly there is an aspect of creativity linked with what Jung calls the 'collective unconscious', with a shared, inherited recollection of experiences going back to the childhood of human history. We know that modern cultural man, European man ('mythless' man, to use a favourite term of Gottfried Benn's) has repressed the experiences of his collective unconscious. But the archetypes remain inextinguishable, lurking in a corner of his imagination, waiting for the moment that will summon them to the light.

Are there archetypes in music? Are there basic sound experiences, rhythm experiences, melody experiences? Comparative musicology has yet to answer this question. It seems that primitive men first made music in a variety of ways, sometimes making purely rhythmical noises, sometimes singing single notes or intervals. At a later stage, however, we find striking similarities: so striking in fact that almost identical musical shapes can be found in Asian Turkey and Hungary, in Arabia and Scotland, and even in Brazil and among the gipsies of Russia.

Nor is this all: there are close analogies between forms of organisation of musical materials at almost all stages of cultural development. The prototype scale-structure we mentioned in chapter 2 is a case in point: the pentatonic scale, a five-note scale without semitones, composed of whole tones and minor thirds arranged in irregular fashion. It occurred in China in 2000 BC and is found in Africa and Polynesia.

All pentatonic melodies have small cells comprising three notes within the interval of a fourth, i.e. whole-tone intervals alternating with minor thirds. Some surviving remnants of the pentatonic legacy can still be found in European folk-song, particularly that of the Balkans. The first modern composers to use them in their works were Bartók and Kodály. In 1905 they made the first of their adventurous journeys into the Hungarian interior and to other countries of south-eastern Europe, visiting the peasants of remote areas still untouched by modern civilisation. Armed with Edison phonographs and wax cylinders, they recorded the songs that were sung to them, transcribed them into modern notation, cataloguing and classifying them in groups according to their relationships and melodic structure, and so established a typology of Hungarian dances and songs that has been of the utmost scientific importance.

In 1906 Kodály received the degree of Doctor of Philosophy for a thesis on strophic form in Hungarian folk-song. He had found traditional Hungarian melodies in which the pentatonic scale was preserved, sometimes in its purest form and sometimes with extra notes as embellishments. Kodály used one of the most beautiful of these melodies, the Song of the Peacock (symbolising liberation), as the theme of his *Variations on a Hungarian Folk-Song* (1938–9). The highly skilled transformations of the melody in this work are a tribute to Kodály's encyclopaedic knowledge of its ethnological relations and similarities to the melodies of other peoples, including distant Mongolian tribes and the Finno-Ugrian Votyaks and

Kodály (1882–1967), with his wife and Bartók (1881–1945) in Budapest, circa 1910. Their Balkan journeys in search of folk-song provided valuable material of a scientific kind, and also personal inspiration for their own compositions. Wide interest in folk-music followed with similar productive results in European countries as well as in the Americas.

153

Cheremis not far from Kazan. Kodály relates how he once conducted his Variations in Moscow. Afterwards an old Mari (a Cheremi) came up to him and said 'But that was our song', proof for Kodály that the song was over fifteen hundred years old.

Bartók also, particularly as a young composer, took over folk-tunes unchanged or with little alteration and built piano pieces from them, as in the *Improvisations on Hungarian Peasant Songs*. We need only consider a work by Kodály inspired by folk-music alongside one similarly inspired by Bartók to see how much compositional freedom a composer can retain in a folk-song style, for all the apparent restrictions. Kodály has a feeling for orchestration that produces highly sensuous sonorities; he dwells voluptuously on chords which envelop each note of the melody in Debussyian fashion, though the music is given a quite new and individual flavour by its Hungarian spicing. Bartók's style, on the other hand, is governed essentially by melody; chords are formed as synthetic products of the melodic intervals, almost without regard for conventional beauty or harmonic logic.

When the *Improvisations* appeared in 1920, Bartók, the author of detailed, comprehensive and scholarly studies of Hungarian and Rumanian folk-music, emerged as a leading advocate of folk-music, particularly with regard to its applications in contemporary music. He wrote an article for Hermann Scherchen's Berlin journal *Melos* entitled 'The influence of folk music on modern art music', in which he maintained:

Pure folk-music first came to have an overwhelming influence on our art-music at the end of the nineteenth century and the beginning of the twentieth. The first examples we should note are the works of Debussy and Ravel, which were permanently, and to some extent decisively, influenced by the folk-music of Eastern Europe and the Far East. This is even more the case in the work of Stravinsky and Kodály: the oeuvre of each composer is an outgrowth of the folk-music of his native land, almost an apotheosis of it (e.g. Stravinsky's *Sacre du printemps*). . . . Let one typical example suffice: Stravinsky's *Pribaoutki*. Here the vocal parts consist of motifs that are . . . without exception imitations of motifs from Russian folk-music. The . . . shortness of the motifs, which are all quite tonal when considered separately, makes possible an instrumental accompaniment consisting of a number of superimposed sound-surfaces which closely match the character of the motifs and are more or less atonal. The overall effect, indeed, is much closer to atonality than to tonality.

A few years later Bartók could have quoted a much more telling example from Stravinsky: *Les Noces*. This work marks the end of Stravinsky's 'Russian' period. It is typically the music of an exile, an over-compensation for frustrated national feelings on a scale almost unprecedented in its intensity. The score is indeed steeped in the spirit of Russian folk-music, and Stravinsky, magician that he is, reduces the essential characteristic of Russian folk-song to a basic motif derived from even earlier forms of music. The kernel of the work is a single three-note idea: a minor third and whole tone within the interval of a fourth, just like the traditional Hungarian penta-tonic melodies that Bartók employed. The four three-note figures

form the skeleton of almost all the themes of *Les Noces*. Never had such a thorough-going reduction been undertaken. The romantics had used similar melodic cells from Russian folk-songs, but they had always sought to integrate them into the language of Western art music. Even Mussorgsky, who aspired to new principles of harmonisation, thought in terms of accommodation and adjustment.

Both Stravinsky and Bartók had a fundamentally different aim. With them, folk material is incorporated not for its picturesque charm but as part of a new scheme of construction. The separate elements are not integrated but are deliberately kept apart to form sharp contrasts. The New Music based on folk-music is an art of relief forms, not one of coloured surfaces. Hence the technique of harmonisation which Bartók calls 'super-imposed, more or less atonal sound-surfaces'. As we now know, this technique is not

Bartók (1881–1945),
photographed in
Basle in 1936.

atonal, but bitonal, in some cases polytonal, i.e. the tonality of the melodic cells is combined with a contrasting tonality in the accompaniment. Thus, in the case of the three-note figures from *Les Noces* flat and flat are bass notes beneath the tetrachord. Taking minor as the tonality, this makes the bass the semitone adjacent to the tonic or the dominant. This is the same principle of octave-avoidance as we find in Schoenberg and the New Viennese School.

As far as music based on folk-music is concerned, this procedure has a further descriptive significance arising from the familiar phenomenon of 'false' intonation or tuning in folk music, which at first we tend to find disturbing but later come to regard as a characteristic and valuable addition to musical language (compare bagpipe fifths). It is a case of a primitive procedure suddenly reappearing in a context of the utmost sophistication. This, indeed, is the stylistic ethos of *Les Noces*, which Stravinsky later scored in the manner of a Spanish orchestrion, with four pianos, xylophone, timpani and percussion, besides voices.

Shortly after completing *Les Noces* Stravinsky underwent one of his characteristic conversions and entered on his period of Neo-classicism. He became opposed to the whole folk-music philosophy; in this he was in agreement with Schoenberg, although the two composers were farther apart at this time than ever before or since. While Bartók advocated a folk-music approach in contemporary music, Stravinsky wrote, à propos of the Russian group around Balakirev:

The Five persisted in cultivating a nationalistic, ethnographic aesthetic which was basically little different from the spirit that inspired those films of the old Russia of the Czars and boyars. Like the modern Spanish folk-lorists, painters and musicians, they were forever seized by the naive but dangerous ambition to create afresh an art which had been in existence for centuries and which had originated in the instincts and genius of the common people.

Schoenberg's rejection was based on more technical grounds. He condemned

Folklorists who, whether they are forced to (through a shortage of theories of their own) or not (because after all, the available musical culture and tradition could find room even for them) wish to apply to the inherently primitive ideas of folk music a technique that suits only a complicated style of musical thinking.

Both composers failed to perceive that there are recurrences and apparent retrogressions within the long-run periodicity of art which transform the seemingly primitive into the progressive and vice versa. We can now see that their common hostility to folk music was a product of their basic positivist view of the history of music as a story of unbroken, cumulative progress. This view has since been supplanted by new and quite different attitudes.

The discoveries of Bavarian glass painting by the *Blaue Reiter* group in 1910, or of Negro sculpture by modern French painters, are only the most conspicuous symptoms of these new attitudes. The disruption of tonal relationships in modern music paralleled the sixteenth-century transition from the church modes to major-minor tonality. And this latter situation seems to have been ana-logous in turn to the supersession, not easily dateable, of penta-tonicism by six- and seven-note scale-systems. It does not take much imagination to picture these historical changes as a spiral stretching far back into the past. There is the further point, discussed earlier, that compared with earlier periods, Western music grew increas-ingly poor in rhythm and metre between the era of mensural notation and the full flowering of Classicism.

Folk-music elements do not occur in Bartók or early Stravinsky as mere quotations. They are integral features, not alien bodies, despite the technique of strict separation of elements that is used. This is not a kind of romantic musical nationalism, with the 'collec-tive' folk material preserved in a kind of 'individualist' art-music nature reserve; it is a quite new phenomenon, a use of relief tech-nique in which the future and the mythical past are merged in a combination of 'some day' and 'once upon a time'.

The late works of Janaček are another striking and graphic

example of a synthesis of 'collective' and 'individualist' material, this time within the field of Czech and Moravian music. Janáček, the oldest of the great musical innovators of the twentieth century, was born in 1854 and grew up in a milieu in which a Slav folk-culture was more alive than in many other areas. Relatively late in his career he evolved a style in which modality and pentatonicism are blended with harmonies built on whole tones and fourths as naturally and easily as if all were products of the same *Zeitgeist*. This was long after his successful opera *Jenufa*, completed in 1902.

Like Bartók and Kodály (and unlike Stravinsky), Janáček was a student of folk-music, and he made a habit of listening to bird-song and the rhythms of human speech. These diversified observations enabled him to build up a method of operatic composition that came to its fruition in the magnificent works *Katya Kabanova*, *The Cunning Little Vixen*, and *The House of the Dead*. Among the melodic types he found in Moravian folk song were the three-note figures we observed in Stravinsky and the Hungarians.

The formula Janáček found in the first movement of the *Sinfonietta* (1925) for integrating three-note motifs of this kind was both age-old and modern. Certain musical shapes recur repeatedly in his works: shapes which are based not so much on the classical sense of tonality as on pentatonicism and church modality and which, as in Debussy and Ravel, avoid the cadence via the leading note. This is particularly true of the *Glagolithic Mass*, which seems to hark back to heathen, almost prehistoric, archetypes. Janáček had an intuitive sense for the similarities between all types of folk-song. He wrote 'modern' music, but he also believed that modern music needed to be revitalised by folk-music. He expressed this belief in a speech in London in 1926 at a concert of English folk song:

Folk-song is a unity: it is the expression of men who know only the culture of God, not an alien, inflicted culture. I believe that a time will come when all art music will spring from a common folk source, when we shall embrace each other in these created works by the shared experience of folk-song. Folk-song binds together all mankind in *one* spirit, *one* happiness, *one* salvation.

However, the folk-music of Spain and the Iberian peninsula is as rich in preserved archaic, 'collective' forms as Slav and Balkan music, and yet has very little in common with them. There are great ethnical and cultural differences between the various regions of the peninsula, from Portugal in the south to the Basque region in the north, where the people and customs are the same as those on the French side of the border. It is the music of Andalusia that has always seemed most typically 'Spanish' – this even before *Carmen*. The best-known types of folk-song, though not the oldest, come from Andalusia: the *cante hondo* and the *cante flamenco*. The *hondo* is of ancient origin, emotional, melancholy, almost tragic, and was probably developed by Sephardic Jews and gypsies; the *flamenco*, descended from the *hondo*, is a gypsy combination of song and dance, generally extremely lively and sometimes bordering on the orgiastic. Both types make considerable use of falling tetrachord figures, e.g. the notes B – A – G – F sharp.

All melodic shapes based on tetrachords are very ancient in origin. This particular form with a bottom interval of a semitone, the Dorian mode of the Greeks or the medieval Phrygian mode, has far-reaching structural applications.

Some elements of northern Spanish and Basque music go back to very ancient roots. The musicologist Curt Sachs tried to show that the fandango was descended from Phoenician forms. The Basques have evolved a characteristic sonority for the fandango by playing it on the xistu (a small wooden flute) and side-drum. Spanish musicians clearly feel a cultural affinity with the Arabs. The poet Lorca also drew attention to Eastern influences in his observations on the *cante hondo*. Lorca, incidentally, gained a special and deep understanding of gypsy lyric poetry, and not only from a literary point of view. During the twenties he became friendly with the composer Falla, who transported important elements of Andalusian folk song into contemporary music.

Apart from Albeniz and Pedrell, the chief representatives of Spanish musical nationalism, it was French composers – Chabrier, Debussy and Ravel – who used Spanish folk-music to greatest

Falla (1876–1946) used Andalusian folk-song and gypsy-style
accompaniment to create universal and yet totally
Spanish images in his ballets *El Amor Brujo* and
The Three-cornered Hat. Moorish affinities are clearly
felt by Spanish musicians, but there are hints at
far earlier links with Greek and Phoenician times.

advantage. Albeniz sought to tap the vast resources of Spanish regional music. His *Suite espagnole* includes some of the most important song and dance forms, from the serenade of Granada by way of the *jota* of Aragon to the 5/8 *zortziko* of the Basques. Falla was more selective in this respect, more particularly attached to the *flamenco* and *hondo* of Andalusia, but he was also the much stronger creative personality. In his Spanish folk-songs he often uses the *polo* form, a most interesting dance which, like the Czech *furiant*, consists of alternating 3/4 and 6/8 metres in hemiola rhythm.

Even more than Albeniz, Falla uses the piano to simulate the sound of the guitar, which with the castanets is the chief instrument in southern Spain. Gypsy songs with guitar accompaniment are the source of inspiration of Falla's ballet-pantomime *El Amor Brujo*. Here song and dance, the universal foundations of folk music, are reduced to stylised formulae and moulded into a work of art that spans the whole gamut from tragedy to intoxication. In the famous Fire Dance we once again find melodies bridging the tetrachord, in this case that falling from G to D with additional chromatic notes. Modal and Greek scale-patterns are also common in Spanish music, but pentatonicism is rare. It has clearly either been displaced by later seven-note scales or has merged into them as a result of developments in melodic writing.

Latin American music has been within the sphere of influence of Spain and Portugal since the sixteenth century, without however losing its own distinctive character. Indeed, there have been instances of feedback, with dance forms crossing the Atlantic and then returning home. Such was the history of the habañera, which originated in Spain but assumed its final shape in Central America and was then brought back to Europe, where Bizet, Ravel and Debussy used it in opera and the concert hall.

The enormous wealth of Central and Southern American folk music has not been exploited by composers or studied scientifically. However, the half-Indian Brazilian composer Villa-Lobos in some of his vast number of works has brilliantly solved the problem of combining the exotic lyricism of his native land with modern compositional techniques. There are some highly original pieces in his piano adaptations of Brazilian children's songs *Cirandas* (1926, such as 'The Battle of the Carnation and the Rose'. The *Choros No. 12* for orchestra also incorporates native folk-material.

An autochthonous folk-music seems to have been most actively preserved in Mexico. Notable composers are Carlos Chavez, the amateur Silvestre Revueltas, victim of an early and tragic death, and the unorthodox sexaganarian Daniel Ayala, who is of Mayan descent and has reworked the ancient pentatonic melodies of his country in novel fashion in his orchestral suite *Tribu*. Revueltas' *Homenaje a Garcia Lorca* transmits a most powerful message. The slow central movement, *Duelo*, is a highly personal version of Milhaud's polytonal treatment of folk-material.

The question whether the latest procedures of modern music, twelve-note and serial techniques, permit the use of folk-material has been answered in varying ways, notably so by the members of the Viennese school themselves. In 1947, a few years before his death, Schoenberg published an essay entitled 'Folkloristic Symphonies' in which he maintained that folk melodies are quite unsuitable for large and more complicated formal structures. He admits that much folk-music is beautiful, especially that of Hungary, but he questions whether it is adequate for the symphonic concept.

However, Schoenberg's own music suggests a somewhat different answer. The third movement of the Suite Op. 29, completed in Berlin in 1926, is a theme and four variations on the melody *Ännchen von Tharau*. (This melody has become a folk-song although it was in fact written by the romantic composer Silcher, whom Schoenberg incidentally treats with some disdain in the aforementioned essay.) The theme is played slowly in E major by the bass clarinet, accompanied in the other parts by the remaining notes of the various forms of the series, grouped in triad-like combinations. The result is a kind of twelve-note polytonality, which produces an effect of fragmentation and ambivalence more curious than organic. One is reminded of Schoenberg's ironic remark on the difference between folk-music and art-music:

Schoenberg's Suite Op. 29:
Ännchen von Tharau is played
on the bass clarinet.

They may not be as different as oil and olive oil or holy water and washing water, but they mix as badly as oil and water.

However, in 1939 in America, thirteen years after the ironic folk-song variations, Schoenberg wrote the sacred work we mentioned earlier, *Kol Nidre*. Here a traditional Jewish melody with oriental and Spanish elements provides a *cantus firmus*. Schoenberg builds up a strict symphonic movement on the basis of the motivic properties of the melody, using the complex techniques typical of his twelve-note compositions. The structure of *Kol Nidre* is not twelve-note, however. The work is tonal, though its tonality is free and rich in chromatic alterations. The deviation from the style of Schoenberg's other compositions written at the same time is remarkable.

Folk-music in two modern settings:
(*below*) The Carinthian folk-tune which
is quoted in Berg's Violin Concerto.
(*right*) An excerpt from Act 1 of
The Mines of Sulphur by Bennett.

The piece is a considerable work of art and yet it lies outside the mainstream of his creation.

Berg's relation to folk-music was very different. Folk-song elements play an important role in both his operas, appearing within diverse compositional contexts. Folk-songs occur within the free-atonal language of *Wozzeck* and variations on a ballad theme by Wedekind within the twelve-note context of *Lulu*.

But the most striking and brilliant amalgamation is found in his last work, the Violin Concerto. With a clearly programmatic intention Berg here uses a Carinthian *Ländler*, an Alpine yodel song in a primitive species of tonality. The melody consists of six notes. Berg writes it in G flat major and gives it a harmonic basis alternating between G flat major and C major plus the principal steps of the C major scale. This is a bitonal procedure: it enables Berg to bring in the remaining six notes of the series in the accompaniment, in the manner of Schoenberg's variations in the Suite. Berg is at the same time so little bound by orthodoxy that he holds over the note A. The meaning of this becomes clear only in the later course of the work.

In this instance the quotation is so unforced that the folk theme does not seem an extraneous element. Strictly speaking, of course, many traditional songs written in a pentatonic or modal system cannot be harmonised even in major-minor terms. But, as in tonal music, melodic shapes can be formed in twelve-note music into which folk material can be woven. Indeed, for this purpose it is the

Lento e dolce (♩=63)

"The wind dok blow To-night, my love and a few small drops of rain.

ne-ver had but one true love, in cold grave he was lain—

oldest melody-types such as chromatically filled tetrachords that are particularly serviceable, certainly more serviceable than later, or indeed romantic, types of folk-song.

As far as recent German twelve-note music is concerned, Wolfgang Fortner and Hans Werner Henze have particularly contributed towards a solution of these problems. The *cante hondo* in Act 1 of Fortner's *Bluthochzeit* is a more characteristic example than the interludes in the same opera, though these too are steeped in Spanish folk idiom in their own unusual way. Many recent works by younger composers indicate the stimulating effect that folk-metres and rhythms have had on contemporary music.

Among English composers, Richard Rodney Bennett has shown how folk melodies may be incorporated into a highly modern musical language in this opera *The Mines of Sulphur*. His exemplar here has been Benjamin Britten, who blends a folk-song spirit into many of his melodies with great subtlety, almost intuitively.

Folk-music and exoticism have held an assured place in French music since Debussy and Ravel. Both composers were profoundly impressed in their youth by the performance of oriental and north African music at the Paris World Exhibition of 1889, was reflected in the penatonic and exotic melodies of their children's pieces, *Children's Corner* (1906–8) and *Ma Mère l'oye* (1908). Moreover, Debussy's whole-tone scales are rationalised or stylised versions of oriental scales such as the Javanese *slendro* and *pelog*, whose intervals do not coincide with our own tempered scales. But

Messiaen's uses of rhythm:
(*below*) A section of the 'Danse de la fureur, pour les sept trompettes' from *Quatuor pour la fin du temps*, with a non-retrogradable (i.e. palindromic) rhythm.
(*right*) Rhythmic modes in *L' Ange aux parfums*. Example (b) is a retrograde of (a), while (c) is a non-retrogradable structure, itself built out of three symmetrical non-retrogradable cells.

apart from their life-long interest in the mysteries of non-European systems, both composers were highly susceptible to all kinds of European folk music, not least the music of Spain and Andalusia that had already fascinated the pre-impressionist generation in France. Many of Debussy's piano pieces have a Spanish character – *La Soirée dans Grenade* from *Estampes* (1903), *La Puerta del vino* from the second set of *Préludes* (1913) – not to mention the orchestral suite *Ibéria* (1906–8). They are matched by Ravel's works of his 'Spanish year', the opera *L'Heure espagnole* and the orchestral rhapsody. Debussy also frequently drew on the resources of French folk-song, showing a special preference for children's songs, such as *Nous n'irons plus au bois* in *Estampes*, *La petite bergère* in the ballet *La bôite à joujoux* (1913) and others. Ravel filled several volumes with arrangements of folk-songs from different countries, Italian, Hebrew, Scottish, Flemish and Russian. His own native Basque

folk-music is also reflected in the melodies and rhythms of some of his works.

The most individual treatment of exotic music in the Ravel generation was by Maurice Delage. He was particularly fascinated by the music of India, and his *Quatre poèmes hindous* (1912) were a sophisticated attempt to transplant Indian melodies and rhythms into contemporary musical language.

This brings us to Messiaen's investigations into Indian music. In his inspired, highly original text-book *Technique de mon language musical* (1944) Messiaen discusses various types of Indian rhythm. On the basis of *talas* – rhythm-patterns whose variation is an important element in classical Indian music – he builds up a kind of serial rhythmic technique. In this technique non-invertible or non-retrograde rhythms which read the same both backwards and forwards) and the *valeur ajoutée* (non-symmetrical increases of

Copland (b. 1900), perhaps the most immediately 'American' composer of this century, reveals both jazz and folk-music indebtedness in *Rodeo*, *Appalachian Spring* and *El Salon Mexico*. He can also write in a dissonant, non-popular language, proof of the concern for vitality and experiment which has marked his work as pianist, lecturer, writer and conductor.

duration-values) play an important role. He also analyses Indian melody-types (*ragas*), and a variation technique derived from them is a feature of his distinctive method of melodic construction. The organ piece *L'Ange aux parfums* (a movement from the first book of *Les Corps glorieux* of 1933) uses this technique.

In later works Messiaen has also worked with the music of the Indians of South America, as in the cyle of love songs *Harawi* (1944), based on Peruvian sources. André Jolivet, a friend and fellow-member of the 'Jeune France' group, also worked with exotic material and primitive forms in the piano work *Mana* (1935) and related works, such as the five *Incantations* for flute (1936) and the five *Danses rituelles*. Jolivet has a vague, elusive vision of a synthesis of Eastern and Western thought through music.

Composers from countries other than France were also exploring exotic music before the First World War. The English composer Cyril Scott drew on oriental models in his piano suites, particularly on the music of India and China. In Russia the use of exotic idioms by 'the Five', Rimsky-Korsakov especially, made a strong impression on Alexander Tcherepnin. His investigations into Chinese music and his experiments with polyrhythmic complexes and nine-note scales took him back quite independently to the same sources as Messiaen.

Another strand in the tangle of non-European influences on modern music has been the impact of jazz. Jazz has made an important contribution to the rejuvenation of European musical language, ever since the ragtimes and cakewalks of Debussy and Satie before the First World War and the great flood of jazz-inspired compositions after 1918. A composer as much-travelled stylistically as Stravinsky has crossed its path at various interesting points. In his *Ragtime* for eleven instruments (1918) and the *Piano-Rag Music* composed for Artur Rubinstein in 1919 he exploited with great ingenuity the rhythmic and instrumental manner then current in American dance music; similarly in the *Ebony Concerto* written seventeen years later for the Woody Herman band. Jazz has also left its imprint on American music itself, in such diverse works as

Louis Gruenberg's lyrical cantata *The Creation* and a rhythmic composition like George Antheil's *Ballet mécanique*. Later American composers have gone back to native folk music; Aaron Copland's *Appalachian Spring*, and *Tales of the Countryside* by the erstwhile innovator Henry Cowell, are notable examples.

Modern German and Austrian composers before the First World War regarded folk-music and exotic music as the resort of reactionaries. In the *Harmonielehre* Schoenberg attacked Busoni and the critic Georg Capellen, author of the book *Ein neuer exotischer Musikstil* (1906). He derided the catch-phrase 'Back to nature' and professed amazement that 'a Debussy should have hoped to find Nature away from the paths that Art has already left behind, in the wilderness remote from Art where only the backward and the lawless dwell.'

The Hindemith generation thought otherwise. Hindemith used traditional folk-songs in his Viola Concerto of 1937 (*Der Schwanendreher*), including the song which gives the work its title and provides the theme for the variations of the last movement. Schoenberg, too, had always emphasised that variation technique calls for simpler thematic material than symphonic writing. In France it was the 'Six' group that led the movement back to folk-song sources in the twenties. Milhaud repeatedly used themes and rhythms based on folk-songs and dances, both in the Brazilian works of the war years (e.g. *Saudades do Brasil*) and in later works like the *Suite provençale* of 1937. Poulenc, who in Ravel's neat phrase 'invents his own folk tunes', used French folk-song themes in the ballet *Les Biches* (1924), and Honegger used Swiss tunes in his *Deliciae Brasilienses* (1947).

In the Soviet Union composers are officially encouraged to draw on the resources of Russian folk-music. Nearly all composers have taken up the invitation at one time or another. Shostakovich has done so several times since the Fifth Symphony. Prokofiev's *Peter and the Wolf* has been exceptionally successful.

The compositions of Aram Khachaturian are predominantly based on folk-music, with a strong element of exoticism. The ballet *Gayane* and other works embody his native Armenian music and have brought him considerable fame, although not even this prevented him from being accused of formalism alongside Shostakovich and Prokofiev in 1948.

It is fashionable in certain avant-garde circles today to denounce the use of folk-music and exotic music as a deviation from the only true path. This view squares with that of the futurists of 1910. Even Marinetti, who was to become a pro-fascist, rejected all attempts to reconcile modern music and folk-song because he claimed they were

Poulenc (1899–1963), as drawn by Cocteau.
The character of his flowing, witty music is
well caught; to show him 'vamping' as a
cabaret pianist is neither malicious nor unfair,
for many of his works (written mostly for the
piano) use popular tunes in parody style.

contrary to technology and urban life. The composers of our own time have no profound intellectual reasons to offer. They have rather found that gulfs in art are much harder to bridge than to ignore. Merely to retreat into isolation and esotericism is to shy away from decisions than can be taken only by those who have a deeper understanding of the relations between art and the cultural situation.

This should not be misunderstood. The ivory tower is the appropriate dwelling for those contemporary composers who have greater claims to consideration. No one should make modern music easy to listen to and to understand by providing listeners with short cuts. Injecting music with songs and dance rhythms would be as inartistic and misguided as daubing abstract paintings with representational images. A *reversion* to folk-music is impossible in any case, because a notion of reversion presupposes a notion of progress and this has for long been discredited. Folk music has to be justified by avant-garde music, not vice versa. If we equate or seek to equate culture with abundance, we must come to terms with the multiplicity that ensues. Contemporary music was given a start in this respect by some composers of the older generation, particularly Bartók and Kodály, Stravinsky and Janáček, Falla and Villa-Lobos. Their example has already proved beneficial and will remain so. Recent developments in modern music seem to be bringing together methods of composition which even a generation ago would have been considered quite incompatible. Serial composers, notably Boulez and Nono, have used techniques that have been inspired by non-European sonorities and rhythms. There have been many interesting attempts in modern Japanese music to achieve a synthesis of native traditions and contemporary techniques. Yoritsune Matsudaira in particular is typical of a whole generation. Toshiro Mayuzumi's *Nirvana Symphony* is a more recent work that achieves this synthesis on a high level of technical accomplishment. Other composers from the Far East, such as the Korean Isang Yun, now resident in Berlin, are also working on similar lines.

The Inter-American Music Festival at Caracas in 1966 forcibly demonstrated how far young Latin American composers are now

9 Technical sound-material

In 1907 Busoni referred to his *Sketch of a New Aesthetic of Music* to an electrical musical instrument called the Dynamophone. This instrument was invented by Dr Thaddeus Cahill and discussed in McClure's Magazine in July 1906, where it was said to be able to produce any combination of notes and overtones at any dynamic level. Busoni was led to hope that here might be the means of putting music on a fully scientific basis:

> Since pitch depends on the number of vibrations and since the apparatus may be set to any number desired, an infinite gradation of the octave can be achieved by the simple expedient of moving a lever corresponding to the pointer of a dial. Only after a long period of careful experimentation and training of the ear will this unfamiliar material become a useful tool of the art of the future.

The German phonetician Dr Werner Meyer-Eppler wrote in 1949 that the Dynamophone was built on the lines of the geared generators used in communications systems and was used to broadcast concerts over telephone lines. Timbres were produced additively; the instrument was related to the later Hammond Organ, but weighed over two hundred tons and looked like the engine room of a ship.

The history of the new method of producing notes and chords by scientific means was a combination of theory and practical experiment. Nineteenth-century physicists were already conversant with certain of the laws relating to the structure of sound. The overtone series and the disposition of the overtones are important factors, though they do not provide a complete explanation. But the fact that a sound could be broken down into its smallest constituent parts did not mean that composite sounds could be produced. Generators had to be invented capable of manufacturing these acoustical atoms. Today there exist a considerable number of instruments for producing sounds electronically. They are divided into two classes: impulse generators, and continuous or permanent sound generators, of which latter there are six different types. With such generators certain acoustical phenomena can be created to which traditional instruments have no access: so-called pure sine waves or 'sinus-tones', i.e. musical sounds without overtones. For the purposes of practical work with sine waves we then need further pieces of equipment: an amplifier, a loudspeaker and a means of sound-distortion.

There were various important landmarks in the development of electronic means of producing sounds. In 1927 the Aetherophone invented by the Russian scientist Leon Theremin attracted some public attention. Theremin had been giving concerts in Russia on instruments of his own invention since 1920. He demonstrated an electronic organ in Leningrad in 1925 and after 1927 gave concerts before bewildered audiences in Germany, France and America. An important feature of the method of frequency determination on his instrument was the distance between an antenna and the player's hand moving freely in space: the closer the hand to the antenna, the lower the sound.

The German teacher Jörg Mager (1880–1939) had experimented with techniques of electronic sound production before the First World War. In 1926 he constructed his Sphärophon, which was demonstrated the same summer at the Donaueschingen Chamber-music Festival. Since 1931 an electronic instrument of Mager's has been used for the bells in *Parsifal* at Bayreuth.

In France in 1928 the composer and teacher Maurice Martenot constructed a manually operated electronic instrument called the Ondes Martenot, which has since been successfully used in compositions by Honegger, Jolivet, Messiaen and others.

An instrument based on somewhat different principles was the Trautonium, developed at the Berlin Hochschule für Musik by the German engineer Friedrich Trautwein and first demonstrated in Berlin in 1930. Trautwein had the backing of the director of the Hochschule, Georg Schünemann, who had created a broadcasting research unit at the college in 1928, and he was thereby able to collaborate with a number of composers. The most prominent of these was Hindemith, whose Concertino for Trautonium and string orchestra (1931) was performed in Munich with great success. The Trautonium was later perfected by a pupil of Hindemith, Oscar Sala, and is still in use in broadcasting and films.

In the middle twenties some composers began to investigate the possible uses of gramophone records as a means of creating new kinds of music. Various experiments were conducted at the Bauhaus in Weimar: scratching records so as to alter rhythms, playing them backwards, or cutting them eccentrically so as to produce howling *glissandi*. Hindemith and Ernst Toch wrote pieces for gramophone records, and also for mechanical pianos and organs. Stravinsky played some of his own works for the mechanical piano of the Paris firm Pleyel. At first there were no links between these experiments and the work on electronic instruments. Both developments, however, showed how profoundly the imaginations of composers had been stirred and disturbed by the new technical media.

A few years after the Second World War Pierre Schaeffer in Paris revived the Italian futurists' attempt to find applications in music for mechanical and everyday noises. Schaeffer made gramophone records of a variety of noises and musical sounds and manipulated them in different ways so that their character was drastically altered. Canonic and polyphonic forms could be produced by using three gramophones at once. All further plans, however, were frustrated by the mechanical and technical limitations of gramophone records. Only when tape recording was introduced in 1950 did genuinely productive and diversified work become possible. Schaeffer christened his brand-new art-form *musique concrète*. With a colleague, Pierre Henry, and various other composers he produced a number of works including the *Symphonie pour un homme seul* and the opera *Orphée*, which was put on at Donaueschingen in 1953.

The range of acoustical materials available to *musique concrète* is virtually unbounded. It takes in the vast palette of noises which the bruitists had attempted to explore methodically, as well as instrumental and vocal musical sounds. When manipulated the sounds and noises are altered so completely that their origins can no longer be recognised. Even the simple device of playing a sound backwards makes a bewildering difference. A normal note on the piano is loudest at the moment of being struck and then gradually dies away, i.e. it is an example of a *diminuendo*; when played backwards it steadily increases in volume till it reaches its maximum dynamic level and then breaks off: in other words it becomes a *crescendo*. Then again, tape speeds can be accelerated or slowed down so that frequencies rise or fall. Filters can be used to eliminate given frequency maxima and minima. Tapes can be cut and reassembled (by splicing) in new combinations. Several tape recorders can be used at once.

At about the same time, in 1950, work in electronic music began in Cologne. The theoretical premises had been laid down by Meyer-Eppler at the Bonn University Institute for Phonetics and Communications Research. The first compositional results, still somewhat unformed, were shown at the International Ferienkurse für Neue Musik in Darmstadt in 1951. They differed from *musique concrète* in that at first only electro-acoustically produced sounds were used. The moving spirit behind the experiments was the musicologist and composer Dr Herbert Eimert, who has also made important studies in the methodology and aesthetic theory of the new method of composition. While drawing a fundamental distinction between *musique concrète* and electronic music, Eimert has listed twelve techniques the two methods have in common:

1 Superposition of sounds;
2 two musically identical tapes can be played in succession (canon);
3 tapes can be cut and spliced (reassembled) in any chosen order;
4 regulation of dynamic intensities;
5 rhythm patterns can be created by translating durations into tape lengths in centimetres;
6 speed changes;
7 retrograde forms;
8 tape-loops (*ostinati*);
9 use of sound tape and blank tape in any chosen order;
10 sound fading in order to produce transitions of timbre;
11 sounds can be faded out;
12 distribution via several loudspeakers, so that the sound 'wanders'.

It is clear that with these experiments the doors were opened onto a new and unexplored world of sound. Early Western music centred round the human voice. The introduction of instruments marked the beginning of a new epoch. Instruments first appeared in thirteenth-century sacred music, but they did not then have distinctive forms and functions and were used only as occasional substitutes for voices. Instrumental music proper, with its own forms equal in status to those of vocal music, began to emerge about 1600. After 1750 instrumental music had a clear predominance over vocal music.

We can thus speak of two eras in the history of music, the vocal and the instrumental. In the vocal era the musician was his own instrument. Instruments brought in a new technical factor: mechanical possibilities increased, and dynamic and frequency ranges were expanded. This gave rise to new and larger-scale forms of expression, although the process of expression itself became more and more dissociated from human beings. Different instruments themselves have different degrees of dissociation in this sense. Keyboard instruments are highly mechanised, particularly the organ, where the player can influence the tone only by regulating the stream of air entering the pipes. Wind players have the closest physical contact with their instruments; string players can approximate to the desired tone quality by using finger pressure and bow movements.

Electronic music constitutes a third era within this scheme. It stands in the same relation to instrumental music as instrumental music to vocal music. Electronic sounds are not created 'naturally', as even the sounds of the organ still were; the frequencies are a product of science. This non-natural derivation has always been used as a weapon in the arguments about electronic music. There is no doubt that the subjective factor that dominated music for so long in the name of 'emotional expression' is now close to extinction. The potential goal of music produced in the test tube is dehumanisation. Its tendency is towards objectivity.

Some may see the exclusion of human beings from the process of producing sounds as evidence of the death of art and the triumph of technology over culture. But there is also room for hope that the newly-developed possibilities in sound will open up a realm of new musical forms, as well as endow vocal and instrumental music with fresh inspiration and vitality. This would vindicate our comparative scheme given above, in terms of which electronic music is the historical synthesis of organic and mechanical music. At all events, the importance of the new type of music and the new forms and materials it makes possible should not be under-estimated.

Now, more than a decade since their introduction, *musique concrète* and electronic music are no longer regarded as utterly distinct and separate. As early as 1956 the Cologne school dropped their claim to exclusivity on behalf of sounds produced by pure sine-wave generators. Since then there has been no basic conceptual difference between the two movements.

Schaeffer published a history and rule-book of *musique concrète* in 1952. Much of it is written in the form of a journal recording the results of his experiments. He compares his work with that of the chemists and biologists, whose findings have had consequences far bigger than they bargained for. The raw material Schaeffer works with can be drawn from absolutely anywhere. It can be human or mechanical in origin and can be combined *qua* sound-object with any and every other sound-object. All such sound-objects have their own distinctive characteristics, according to which their ordering and selection in work is determined. Schaeffer's book, *À la recherche d'une musique concrète*, begins with a chronicle of the earliest experiments of January 1948. The main subsequent landmarks are as follows:

1948: The first primitive gramophone-record studies, an *Etude aux chemins de fer*, an *Étude aux tourniquets* and an *Étude aux casseroles*, were made. The Techniques used were at first extremely simple. A 78 rpm record was played at 33 rpm; Schaeffer found that this made train noises sound like a blast furnace. A cough on an abortive recording by Sacha Guitry provided a valuable piece of raw material. It was combined with the rhythm of a motor-boat engine, an American accordion record and a priest's song from Bali. 'Ainsi naissent les classiques de la musique concrète' notes Schaeffer. These 'classics' were broadcast by French Radio on 5 October 1948 as a 'concert de bruits'. The public was alarmed.

1949: Collaboration began between Schaeffer, Jaques Poullin and Pierre Henry. Schaeffer graphically describes the difference in genesis between traditional music and 'concrete' music. The former is conceived in the mind, written down and then performed on instruments. The latter starts with given acoustical elements, derived from any chosen sound-source; they are fitted together directly by a process of experimental montage, and then (notation no longer being relevant) reproduced as sound.

After various preliminary steps Schaeffer and Henry produced the *Symphonie pour un homme seul*, which later became famous and was turned into a ballet by Maurice Béjart. The work is in several sections and, as its name suggests, it is based on the sounds and noises that a man can produce by himself without the aid of instruments. Mechanical sounds are also brought in, however, and within either category both pitched sounds and noises are used. Schaeffer catalogues the sounds as follows:

Human sounds:	*Non-human sounds:*
Different kinds of breathing	Footsteps etc.
Vocal fragments	Knocking on doors
Shouting	Percussion
Humming	Prepared piano
Whistled tunes	Orchestral instruments

(The 'prepared piano' is an invention of the American composer John Cage, whom Schaeffer met in 1949. Objects of metal, rubber and other materials are fitted between the piano's strings so that its sound is drastically altered.)

1950: The introduction of tape recording stepped up the technical possibilities of manipulating acoustical material. Developments were rapid. There was a period of frantic experimentation. Schaeffer and his colleagues were soon treating the names of their brain-children as jokes, e.g. Henry's *Concerto des ambiguités* or the *Bidule en ut* by Schaeffer and Henry. In March there were public performances of *musique concrète*, including one at the Sorbonne.

and it was also used as incidental music for a play by Adamov, *La grande et la petite manoeuvre*.

1951: The Paris broadcasting system installed a specially equipped studio for Schaeffer and his colleagues. Schaeffer gave a lecture-demonstration on his work at the Darmstadt Ferienkurse. Young French composers, including Pierre Boulez, Michel Philippot and Jean Barraqué, and the Germans Hermann Scherchen and Karlheinz Stockhausen came to work in the studio. The Groupe de recherches de musique concrète was incorporated into the French broadcasting service. Contacts were set up with Olivier Messiaen, Marcel Delannoy, Jean-Jacques Grunewald, André Jolivet, Yves Baudrier and Henri Dutilleux. A. Moles joined the group in a research capacity. He made precise analyses of acoustical phenomena, estimated the total number of pure musical sounds making up music's atomic structure (thirteen million), and also made important contributions in aesthetic theory. Thus, Moles emphasises the *permanence* of a recorded piece of music (plus features added by interpreters); its *reproducibility*, which makes it an object of scientific investigation (whereas formerly all that was possible was a comparison of viewpoints); and its *reversibility* or *invertibility*, which he sees as an incursion of space into time.

Moles and Schaeffer together worked out a kind of primer of *musique concrète*. It contains the first twenty-five words of a vocabulary in which acoustical phenomena are classified according to orders of magnitude and other criteria.

The first sizeable work to result from the experiments of the Paris group was an '*opera concret*', *Orphée*, by Schaeffer and Henry. It had its premiere at Donaueschingen in October 1953, though a shorter version had been put on in Paris two years earlier. Collages of awe-inspiring sonorities and violent outbursts of noise were set against the complete antithesis of arias for two female voices, recitatives with harpsichord accompaniment in the style of Gluck and expressionistic episodes for solo violin.

1954–7: practical work in *musique concrète* went steadily ahead. Well-known composers like Milhaud and Henri Sauguet used it in works written in their own more traditional style. Schaeffer invited Edgard Varèse to work in the studio; he was encouraged to come to Europe by André Malraux, and arrived in Paris in October 1954. There he completed a composition, *Déserts*, combining live sounds and taped *musique concrète*. It was first performed on 2 December at the Théâtre des Champs-Elysées. The programme, conducted by Hermann Scherchen, opened with an overture by Mozart and closed with Tchaikovsky's *Pathétique*. *Déserts* had an angry reception; there was a disturbance in the grand manner which many in the audience compared with the uproar at the premiere of Stravinsky's *Le Sacre du printemps* in 1913.

In 1958 Schaeffer reorganised his methods of composition and his studio. The young composers Luc Ferrari (born 1929) and François-Bernard Mache (born 1935) joined his staff. Yannis Xenakis, somewhat older, a Greek architect and assistant to Le Corbusier, produced his *Diamorphoses* at the studio. The name *musique concrète* was replaced by the more general term *expèriences musicales*. Others to work with Schaeffer during this period were the Bulgarian André Boucourechliev, Luciano Berio and Michel Philippot.

Schaeffer's mature works since 1958 have been founded on new principles. He has renounced the more obvious techniques of distortion and subscribes to an ascetic approach, the results of which he once more calls 'études'. The chief of these is the *Étude aux allures* (1958), which is based on the sound of small hemispheric Chinese bells of bronze. Messiaen has said that the piece is wholly liberated from surrealist agony and literary descriptivism.

During this period the electronic studio at Cologne Radio was set up. It was officially put into operation on 18 October 1951 and was directed until 1963 by its spiritual father Dr Herbert Eimert, and thereafter by his long-standing colleague Karlheinz Stockhausen. In the early days the technical expert Fritz Enkel also worked at the studio, and he built the important control console.

The first compositions, by Eimert and Robert Beyer, were performed at the Cologne New Music Festival in 1953. The equipment used consisted of a monochord on the Trautwein model, a melochord developed by H. Bode having two monaural attachments connected to a manual control, a variable-speed tape recorder, and a four-track tape recorder capable of registering up to four different sets of events at a time. All the apparatus was controlled from the central console. Filters were used to order timbres and to convert them into an element of composition.

These earliest Cologne efforts had a very experimental air. One felt that the composers were feeling their way into unknown territory and that the new discoveries had not yet been given any organised shape. In 1953 and 1954 more finished works by Eimert and Stockhausen were produced and they were brought out on gramophone records by the Deutsche Grammophon Gesellschaft. In 1954 a publication came out entitled *Technische Hausmitteilungen des Nordwestdeutschen Rundfunks* which contained important information on the new techniques.

Stockhausen's *Studie I* was composed in the summer of 1953. It was the first work to be based on sinus-tones, i.e. pure musical sounds (*Töne*) without overtones. Timbres were assembled from the sinus-tones by synthesis. At about the same time Eimert was working on his *Glockenspiel*, which employs so-called 'note mixtures' (*Tongemische*), or composite sounds incorporating nonharmonic overtones. Finally, Stockhausen's *Studie II*, completed early in 1954, used synthetically produced noises.

All these works were the result of an alliance of theory plus practical experiment with a specific method of composition. Eimert and Stockhausen both proclaimed that electronic music had a common intellectual and theoretical basis with the techniques of serial composition that were then being developed. By these techniques was meant an extension, derived somewhat arbitrarily from the works of Webern, of Schoenbergian twelve-tone technique to include aspects of musical sound other than pitch. 'Work and material have the same structure', was the basic rule of Cologne electronic music. This dissociated it from the outset from the phonomontages of *musique concrète*.

Křenek (b. 1900), composer of the jazz-opera *Jonny spielt auf* which fathered a host of successors in the late twenties, has continued to experiment with new techniques throughout a prolific working life. His opera *Der goldene Bock* (1964) used electronic effects pre-recorded for the magical elements.

However, since both the Paris and the Cologne groups (and groups formed later in Milan, Tokyo and elsewhere) operated with the same technical procedures, the effects their music produced were strikingly similar. The unbriefed listener encountering a work by Schaeffer, Henry, Eimert, Beyer or Stockhausen for the first time would take much the same impressions away with him. Far more than any traditional form of music, the pieces evoked associations that the composers had in no way intended. Purely subjective mental pictures suggested themselves: many of the sounds had the effect of auditory spirals or crystals, others were reminiscent of gurgles, air bubbles, giant drops of water and the like. In addition there were unforeseen psychological side-effects: listening rapidly became very exhausting, and after only a few minutes symptoms of fatigue and resistance set in that were clearly quite involuntary.

One composer who was attracted to electronic techniques although a fully developed musical personality, was Ernst Křenek. He got to know the Cologne work in 1955 and at once decided to participate. He described his motives in a short article published in 1956, *De Rebus Prius Factis:*

The composer is interested in the electronic medium for two reasons: firstly, it enables him to extend his control over a region of musical elements which remains inaccessible while he still uses conventional instruments. With the help of the electronic apparatus he can even bring timbres into his constructional design.

The second, more important reason he formulates as follows:

Furthermore, he can realize highly complex time-relationships with a degree of precision that an ensemble of human performers can never be guaranteed to provide, even after strenuous and protracted rehearsal.

Křenek then enumerates the possible methods of combining sinus-tones into composite sounds and committing the combinations directly onto tape. The all-important feature of the technique, as he sees it, is that different musical processes can be synchronised. These exploratory advances into the electronic field were soon followed by an actual work, the Whitsun oratorio *Spiritus Intelligentiae Sanctus* (1955–6), which has also been brought out as a gramophone record. The work, however, is not so much an electronic piece, in the strict sense of the Cologne manifesto of 1953, as a combination of electronically produced sounds with techniques taken from *musique concrète*. Křenek used sound syntheses, note mixtures and noises, but combines them with human voices, a soprano, a tenor and his own speaking voice.

The vocal parts are to some extent manipulated electronically. This was necessary in any case, because Křenek uses an octave of thirteen tempered steps, i.e. intervals smaller than a tempered semitone. The music is syncretistic in character, in that it uses conventional techniques like *Sprechstimme* and single sung phrases directly alongside very unusual kinds of electronic sound-phenomena, notably so-called 'coloured noise'. Coloured noise is a filtered selection of frequencies within a given frequency band, as opposed to 'white noise' which contains all such frequencies. Electronic techniques enable composers to tap the great intermediate realm between noise and musical sound. A continuum in the sphere of colour or timbre, corresponding as it were to the frequency continuum, thus becomes a conceivable possibility. At the close of the oratorio Křenek creates a kind of timbre cadence: as the sounds rise and rise to heights where the ear can no longer follow, new rising levels of sound keep entering from below, so that a sense of acoustical infinity is produced. The literary-cum-religious text (taken from the Bible with additional material by Kierkegaard and Křenek himself) is also subjected to a process of multi-level segmentation by being manipulated in various ways.

The first performance of the work clearly pointed to the possibility of a new type of musico-dramatic form based on electronic techniques. Křenek has since used these techniques in the opera *Der goldene Bock*, which was first performed in Hamburg in 1964. Here the electronic passages, reproduced on tape, are at their most effective when they suggest magic: as in the ram's flight through space and his pursuit by jet plane, the conversations between the dragon and ex-queen Nephele appearing as a cloud, and the barking of the hounds of hell. Significantly, both Křenek's uses of electronic techniques, in 1956 and 1964, have been to suggest the supernatural.

Stockhausen brought out a piece based on the Bible at the same time as Křenek, the *Gesang der Jünglinge*, composed between 1955 and 1956. Here a single boy's voice, both speaking and singing, and used in a great variety of ways, furnishes the basis for the whole composition. Stockhausen writes in a commentary on the piece:

The *Gesang der Jünglinge* combines sung sounds and electronically produced ones (vowel-type sounds, consonant noises; a scale of the intermediary forms of tone-mixtures). Sung noises are individual 'organic' members of the more comprehensive 'synthetic' sound family. At certain points in the composition, the sung sounds become comprehensible words; at various degrees of comprehensibility of the word. Whenever speech momentarily emerges from the sound-symbols in the music, it is to praise God (Daniel 3, 'Song of the Men in the Fiery Furnace'). This work is the first to use the direction of the sounds and their movement in space as aspects of the form. The score calls for five groups of loudspeakers to be set up surrounding the audience. For the gramophone version, the composer has made from the original five-track version a new two-track stereophonic synchronisation.

In 1957 Hermann Scherchen set up an institute of electro-acoustics in Gravesano at which filter techniques and room acoustics were particularly studied. Scherchen brought out a number of gramophone records of the studio's work, ranging from its primitive beginnings to more advanced achievements. The Milan studio has also brought out records of Luciano Berio's *Mutazioni* and Bruno Maderna's *Notturno*, both composed in 1956. In Tokyo Makoto Moroi, Toshiro Mayuzumi and Toru Takemitsu have taken up *musique concrète* and electronic music and their work has also appeared on records.

A special type of electronic composition has been developed by Boris Blacher in Berlin. He worked with Fritz Winckel's technical staff and at first operated with orthodox sounds such as trombone *glissandi*, piano chords and singing. The first results were demonstrated in Berlin in 1963. In 1966 his opera *Zwischenfälle bei einer Notlandung* was given its first performance in Hamburg. Large parts of the score are produced electronically and were played at the performance on a four-track tape recorder over four channels. Blacher exploits the intermediate realm between conventional and electronic sound to create passages of a lyrical and dramatic force rare among earlier composers. His raw materials are human voices and instrumental sounds (e.g. solo violin). As in Stockhausen's earlier *Gesang der Jünglinge* and in later opera and ballet composi-

188

Hiller (b. 1924) seen working here with the Illiac computer which he uses at the University of Illinois' Experimental Music Studio.

tions by the Dutch composer Henk Badings, the manner in which the sound wanders around the theatre is an integral part of the music.

Through Werner Meyer-Eppler the science of phonetics has from the first been connected with communications theory. Work on these lines closely ties up with the species of research which, since Norbert Wiener's book *The Human Use of Human Beings*, has become known as cybernetics. Wiener speaks in his book of a second industrial revolution and a growth of mechanisation such that almost all human work will be taken over by automata.

These new automata are the electronic eye and brain, radar and the like. Many of them are fitted with kinds of sense-organs, enabling them to have, as it were, the reactions of living creatures.

Modern psychology has shown, as Pascal foresaw, that human reactions are partly automatic. Cybernetics goes even further and says that man himself is a complicated message or 'information system'.

In recent years in music there have been growing signs of attempts to exclude human beings, not only from the act of performance, but from that of composition. A composing machine called the Datatron has been built in America and was discussed in the journal *Radio Electronics* in 1957. It is an electronic computer that has been specially programmed to produce melodies. An experiment was carried out, for example, in manufacturing plausible and effective new hit songs. A hundred currently popular tunes were first analysed according to their common features. The songs were seen to consist of between 35 and 60 melody notes, 18–25 of which came in the first section (A), 17–35 in the second section (B), when A and B each consisted of eight bars. Melodic lines consisted regularly of five ascending notes followed by a sixth descending note, or vice versa. This information was then fed into the computer along with some of Mozart's remarks on melodic design and the machine was set to work. Note sequences were chosen at random and could even be determined by telephone numbers. Within an hour the computer had produced four thousand brand-new tunes.

The same principle can be applied to small polyphonic structures. A computer can turn out two-part counterpoint in the style of Palestrina, for example. Chord sequences and rhythmic figures can also be produced quite automatically. The Datatron computer, which was developed by the mathematicians Martin L. Klein and Douglas Bolitho, has not been much exploited since 1956. On the other hand, Professor Lejaren A. Hiller Jr., director of an electronic music laboratory in Urbana, Illinois, U.S.A., experimented with another computer called Illiac in the fifties and gave a lecture on his results at the Darmstadt Ferienkurse in 1963. In the lecture Hiller first drew up a chronological table grouping electronic music into four categories:

1 Music written for electronic instruments (1920 onwards);
2 Electronic music recorded on tape (1948 onwards);
3 Music for electronic synthesisers (1955 onwards);
4 Computer music (1957 onwards);

He then distinguished various stages of development within computer music as such, starting with a Suite for string quartet produced by Illiac, as programmed by Hiller and a colleague Leonard Isaacson. He also mentioned a composition by Yannis Xenakis entitled *ST/10-1 080 262*, and a computer cantata of his own that was written in collaboration with Robert Baker of the University of Illinois. Hiller gave the following 'stylistic sources', as he called them:

1 Conditions established *a priori* by the programmer (counterpoint, rules of harmony, serial techniques, graphical notation, etc.);
2 Statistical conditions (statistics relating to style or based on probability calculations);
3 Styles evolved by the computer itself.

The third source, he claimed, is the most important for composition because it is connected with learning theory.

Some of the works composed by computers have been published. They are no worse than many of the compositions produced by human beings that have been performed at music festivals in recent

10 Mathematics – for and against

Chinese and Greek philosophers were aware of the close connections between music and number. The divided string of the monochord was an important tool of musical theory, and it was known or suspected long before the time of Leibniz that the act of listening to music is a kind of unconscious calculation. Leibniz himself saw the universe as in a state of balance, which he termed 'pre-established harmony' and in which 'bodies act as if (to suppose the impossible) there were no souls, and souls act as if there were no bodies; and yet both act as if each influenced the other'.

It has been disputed from earliest times whether emotion or rationality is of greater importance in music. The defenders of reason have had an easier job than their opponents. They can refer to objective laws, while the latter can appeal only to music's subjective effects. Since the Enlightenment the conviction has grown that the joys of music are a product of the play of reason. Even Wagner, an arch-romantic if there ever was one, wrote to the classicist Hanslick: 'The work of art produced non-consciously belongs to ages far removed from our own.' Alfred Lorenz showed in his analytical studies how heavily Wagner's music-dramas lean on arithmetical calculations of structure. Wilhelm Werker went even further in his theoretical writings, notably in his demonstration of Bach's use of mathematical methods in his fugues (*Studien über Symmetrie im Bau der Fugen des Wohltemperierten Klaviers*, 1922).

The magical attraction of number was immensely more of a reality to men of earlier epochs than it was to those of the nineteenth century, whose artistic theories and techniques still influence most people's attitudes today. Romantic ideology, centreing basically on emotion and its subjective expression and rejecting all forms of objectivity, could have little use for number as a source of artistic inspiration. The romantics may have used the mathematical device of dividing a painting according to the Golden Section, but they had no feeling for number in the absolute or in any symbolic sense: numbers were merely a tool for measuring units. This attitude was a far cry from the medieval view, in which number had a symbolic status over and beyond geometry.

The numerical symbolism of the music of Bach has recently been examined once again, by the Berlin theologian and musicologist Friedrich Smend. He has come to some astonishing conclusions and has convincingly demonstrated by means of many examples that Bach was wholly governed by mathematical considerations and by the symbolic imagery relating to note quantities when he composed.

We have seen that the range of pitches found in nature is limitless (the *glissando* of a howling wind is a graphic illustration). Men have selected a few of the infinite number of possible scale-steps – at first only two or three, then five, then seven, stopping at seven not so much because a seven-note scale is particularly well suited for forming melodies, as because this was the point at which belief or superstition drew some sort of line, and the line was not overstepped for centuries. It cannot be doubted that heptatonicism has mystical and symbolic undercurrents. Nothing else could have prevented men from availing themselves of six-, eight- or nine-note scales if they had so wished. Of course, the connection between number and pitch (or frequency) affects only one dimension of music: its extension in tonal, i.e. intervallic space. Since music occurs in time and is only perceivable at all through time, we shall also need to consider it in its temporal dimension. In this respect music can be seen as an incomparable and unique means of imposing order on time. The temporal dimension is the basis of rhythm, the use of texts, and structural forms.

In 1943 a Russian composer and musicologist called Joseph Schillinger died in New York. He was born in Kharkov in 1895, studied composition in St Petersburg under Nicolai Tcherepnin and Joseph Wihtol until 1917, taught music in Kharkov and Leningrad, and as early as 1918 was appointed dean of the Ukrainian State Academy. In 1927 he was commissioned by the state to write a work for the tenth anniversary of the October Revolution, and he produced a symphonic rhapsody for piano and orchestra entitled *October*. In 1929 he left Russia and settled in the United States. He worked at Leon Theremin's research laboratory in New York until 1932. Between 1932 and 1936 he taught at the New York School for

Social Research and at Columbia University. Later he restricted himself to private tuition. His reputation as a teacher of composition became so widespread that he was able to take a fashionable apartment in Park Avenue, and here his pupils came in great numbers to receive the special brand of artistic panacea he had to offer. As early as 1932 the journal of the League of Composers, *Modern Music*, published his sensational essay *Electricity, a liberator of music*. In 1941 he finished his well-known book *The Schillinger System of Musical Composition*, and in 1942 his *magnum opus*, *The Mathematical Basis of the Arts*. Both were published only after his death.

Schillinger described himself as a scientist of artistic production. He was the most consistent, radical and erudite, as well as the most hopelessly one-sided, of all the romanticisers of technology and the machine.

His belief that artistic creation could be converted into a process of combining mathematically quantifiable factors of production was well matched to the naive rationalism of the modern world. It fell on particularly fertile soil in America. By no means all the composers who came to Schillinger for instruction and advice were beginners; many of them had already 'arrived', particularly those who were composers of light music.

His most notable pupil was George Gershwin. Gershwin came to him as the famous writer of over seven hundred songs, hoping to overcome a temporary loss of creativity. He remained a pupil for four and a half years. For two years, watched over by Schillinger, he worked on the opera *Porgy and Bess*, and it was completed and first performed in Boston in 1935. Schillinger reports how Gershwin was not happy with one of his themes for the opera. He applied the mirror-form technique from Schillinger's musico-technological theory to the theme; the retrograde inversion eventually gave him the characteristic shape he had been searching for. Despite all its intellectual weaknesses, and the occasional pieces of childish positivism (plus a number of mathematical errors), the Schillinger system is the most comprehensive theory yet devised of the role of art in the technological age. It is a particularly rich and flexible example of the

Ravel (1875–1937) and Gershwin (1898–1937), with (at left) the Berlin conductor Fried, a photograph probably taken in Paris in 1928. Ravel greatly influenced Gershwin, and Gershwin's serious works have something of his teacher's nervous rhythms and brilliant orchestral detail.

de-mythologising tendency in modern aesthetics. Its representative force and influence should therefore not be under-estimated, despite all the criticism it has aroused. Even if his books have not become well known – they have been out of print for many years – his portrayal of a huge scheme of formal and mathematical relationships has continued to find adherents until the present day, more than thirty years after his premature death.

What is the substance of his theory, and why is it so persuasive? In the short foreword to *The Mathematical Basis of the Arts* (dated 27 February 1942) Schillinger says that he does not claim to be able to transform the reader into a creative artist. The book's purpose is rather to lay bare the mechanism of creativity as it is revealed in nature and the arts.

> This system, which in a sense is itself a product of creation, i.e. a work of art, opens new vistas long awaiting exploration.

Whereas a scientific theory supplants other scientific theories, only to be itself supplanted by new facts and proofs, his system is able to account for all possible facts and proofs. He puts the date of the oldest branches of his system at 1917, and the most recent at 1932.

The book itself, 696 pages large octavo, is divided into three sections:
1 Science and Esthetics
2 Theory and Regularity and Coordination
3 Technology of Artistic Production.
A large portion of the book is taken up with formulae, diagrams, equations and rows of figures.

Schillinger wants the artist to be able to overcome limitations of history and geography. He wishes to instruct him scientifically in all known and attainable styles and techniques and so lead him to freedom. The heart of the enquiry into science and aesthetics is the chapter entitled 'Nature of Esthetic Symbols', which is concerned with sematics, or the meaning of artistic forms, melody in particular. Schillinger draws attention to the similarity between melody and speech. He defines melody in three ways, physiologically, semantically and musically, and claims that even a poem spoken in a language foreign to the listener constitutes an undeveloped form of music.

The next chapter, on creation and criteria in art, is devoted to what may be termed Schillinger's fundamental thesis, namely that art is the result not of spontaneous creation but of 'engineering', i.e. of planned construction.

The second main section of the book opens with a discussion of the boldly-treated concept of the 'continuum', which is defined as a system of unlimited parameters. Schillinger uses the concept 'parameter' in Einstein's sense: time and space are seen as general parameters, and there are in addition special parameters relating to the elements of each individual art-form.

He then draws up a table of possible individual art-forms, which he claims to be eighteen in number. They are based on the five senses: hearing, feeling, smelling, tasting, and seeing. Their general elements are time and space: their special elements are sound, material, smell, taste, light, colour and surface. Music comes first in the list of possible art-forms. Schillinger gives three parameters relating to audible sound: pitch, dynamic intensity and colour ('character').

How does Schillinger's practical theory of composition work out? It, too, is based on a scientific observation and ordering of symmetries, deviations, row or serial methods, permutations, mirror forms and the like. Mechanical procedures such as doubling and tripling of intervals are shown to lead to drastic alterations of style. An experiment of this kind is carried out on a little melody by Haydn. The melody spans the interval of a fifth, ascending from C to G by way of D and F and then descending back to C by step. When the intervals are doubled the melodic span is of course doubled: the melody runs from C to high D, and the diatonic steps of C major are replaced by the whole-tone scale. Further enlargements of the intervals produce melodic figures reminiscent of Hindemith and Berg, larger ones still of Webern.

Schillinger maintains that the application and combination of

A page from the electronic score of Stockhausen's *Studie II*. Frequencies are drawn along the top area, with line spacing corresponding to the interval $\sqrt[25]{5}$ from 100 to 17200 c.p.s. Overlapping note mixtures are indicated by heavier shading. Volume is marked in the lower area against an intensity scale of decibels between 0 dB and −30 dB.

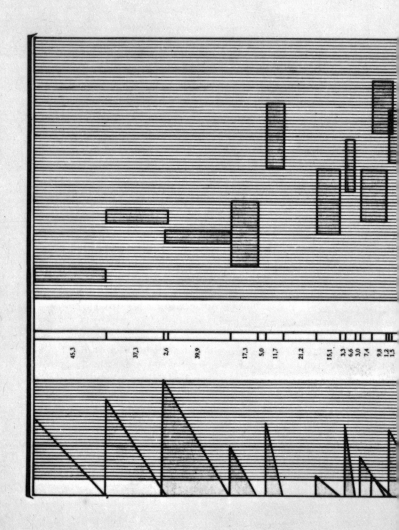

Between the two areas duration is indicated in centimetres, at a tape-speed of 76·2 cms per second. Each change along the time axis is marked by a stroke; note mixture overlays are reckoned as changes also, with their beginnings and endings shown.
The duration of any note mixture is therefore the sum total of all length indications between its beginning and end.

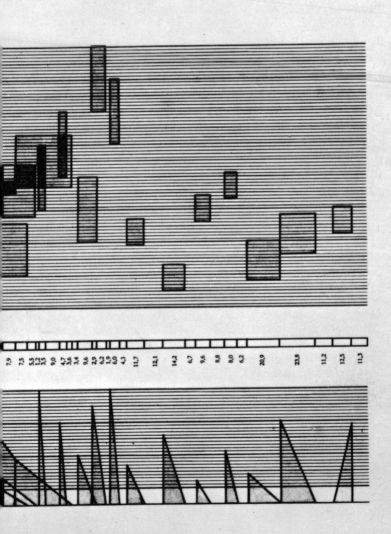

these procedures are an obligatory part of a rationalised system of composition. He cites the three mirror-forms in the F major Two-Part Invention by Bach and is naive enough to comment:

For example, by comparing the music of J.S. Bach with the following illustrations, the full range of what he could have done by using the method of geometrical inversions becomes clear.

This comment shows up with particular clarity the one-sidedness and weakness of Schillinger's system and its rootedness in shallow nineteenth-century positivisim. By being thus confined it is tied to materialism in much the same way as many political panaceas.

Bernard Shaw once said that the Germans never realise it is possible to have too much of a good thing. Schillinger too, the Russian with the German name, overlooks a basic rule that applies to all art in his veritably Faustian urge to exhaust and make explicit the capacities of every conceivable artistic technique. This rule we can call the principle of economy of selection. Bach was as well versed in the possible uses of the three mirror forms of a melody as any Netherlands polyphonist of the fifteenth or sixteenth century. He did not omit to use one or the other of them out of forgetfulness or a defective grasp of the full range of possibilities. He knew that a two-part invention can occupy only a limited amount of space. The ability to make the right choice from the million or more possible forms is a creative secret which cannot be uncovered by science or technology. Here, too, is where the astonishing capabilities of computers prove to have limitations.

The fruitful aspects of Schillinger's system have been fully appreciated by many modern composers. Analysis and synthesis in terms of parameters is a central feature of some serial methods of composition (though the term 'parameter' has not always been correctly used in its original physical and mathematical sense), and selection procedures have played some part in electronic music.

Micro- and macro-forms as described by Schillinger play an important part in the structuring of much contemporary music. Even the notation of electronic works (c.f. the printed scores of

Stockhausen's *Studie II* and Franco Evangelisti's *Incontri di fasce sonore*) goes back to a diagrammatic notation invented by Schillinger and reproduced in his *magnum opus*.

Interestingly enough, this rationalist musical engineer was no champion of modern art. He had hard words to say against those he calls 'ism-makers' in painting, Picasso, Kandinsky, Klee and others. On the other hand, in the appendix to his book he expresses his support for a composition machine built by Theremin called the Rhythmicon, which was able to manufacture rhythms automatically by means of sixteen interchangeable units. Schillinger tells us that it could produce 65,535 rhythmic configurations.

This brings us back full circle to the computer music we described earlier. In actual fact, the dream that man might be a dispensable factor in the creation of music is not as new as might be thought. The scholars of the Baroque era keenly indulged in similar games and speculations. One of the cleverest of them, the Jesuit and natural philosopher Athanasius Kircher, gave an outline in his *Musurgia Universalis* (1622) of an apparatus called the Arca Musarithmica which could turn out compositions by a mathematical process.

As a sublimated expression of the play instinct ideas of this kind have a certain charm and even a measure of relevance to art. They cannot be excluded from a discussion of the growth of Western music, any more than can the alchemists from a discussion of the history of chemistry. The alchemists tried to make gold. We have learned from them and we can also learn from their descendants. But it would be rash to assume that gold will be forthcoming.

Schillinger's name was not mentioned at the Darmstadt Ferienkurse in the fifties. Probably most of the participants had not heard of him. But his style of thinking could be seen in many particulars of the new techniques of composition that were being worked out and applied in Darmstadt at that time. Serial techniques are essentially a systematic transference of Schoenberg's twelve-note technique to elements of musical sound other than pitch. After frequency, the first element to which these techniques were seen to be suited was duration, i.e. the temporal dimension. Metre and rhythm are in fact the most important means apart from pitch of arranging musical sounds into organised shapes. A single note is not a musical element: it qualifies as a possible musical idea only when it joins company with other notes. Berg had already used rhythmic ideas in the form of rows or series in Act 3 of *Wozzeck* and the 'Monoritmica' in *Lulu*. Messiaen took this technique further. The score of the *Quatuor pour la fin du temps*, which was written as early as 1940, includes an outline of his theory of rhythm which he recommends the players to study. One important element of the theory is the so-called 'rhythmic pedal', which Messiaen defines as 'an independent rhythm which is repeated continuously regardless of the rhythms surrounding it'. A seventeen-unit rhythmic pedal of this kind is found in the piano part in the first movement of the quartet, the *Liturgie de cristal*. It is coupled, moreover, with a sequence of twenty-nine chords that is also continuously repeated. Two patterns comprising different numbers of units (17 and 29 in this case) will continue to form new combinations with new points of intersection until the possible permutations are exhausted.

If Messiaen had gone right through with this process of combination the *Liturgie de cristal* would have lasted several hours. He does not, and the movement ends at a point dictated by the other, co-ordinated, events in the clarinet, violin and cello.

In his text-book *Technique de mon langage musical* (1944) Messiaen applies further, predominantly mathematical, methods to musical elements. Thus he derives new scales from the twelve-note tempered semitonal scale. Unlike Busoni in the *Sketch of a New Aesthetic of Music*, he does not base himself on the seven-note norm but groups notes into scales of between six and ten notes. What he is interested in is a principle of artistic economy: a concept of limited transposability.

Traditional major and minor scales can be formed on all twelve degrees, without identical sequences of notes being thereby created. Messiaen uses scales which can be transposed only a limited number of times. He calls them 'modes', numbering them from 1 to 7. Mode 1 is the whole-tone scale, which can be transposed only once without repetitions of sequence. Mode 2 is a sequence of alternating semitones and whole tones, e.g.:

and can be transposed onto two other degrees without repetitions. It has eight notes. Mode 3 has nine notes and can be transposed onto three other degrees:

Mode 7 has ten notes and can be transposed four times:

In the course of his theoretical investigation of these scales (and of non-invertible or non-retrograde rhythms) Messiaen speaks of the 'charme des impossibilités'. Some of the scales are already found in nineteenth-century Russian music, particularly in Rimsky-Korsakov and Scriabin; the whole-tone scale is found as early as Liszt, as well as later in Dukas and Debussy. Messiaen, however, was the first to study the scales methodically, and he has also derived a system of harmony from them which is an important feature of his musical language.

In a context of weakening tonality scales and chords of this kind have an important functional role. They contain an in-built polytonality, as it were, inasmuch as a gravitational pull is exercised by more than one root. Messiaen might have complemented his 'charme des impossibilités' by a 'charme des ambiguités'. The ambiguous character of the modes of limited transposability is a melodic counterpart to the function fulfilled by 'vagrant harmonies', i.e. augmented triads and diminished seventh chords, in the harmonic field.

Messiaen has also been a key figure in the genesis of 'serial' techniques of composition. Pierre Boulez, Jean-Louis Martinet and Serge Nigg have stated that he proposed in 1942 that the rows or series which Schoenberg had applied to pitch and Berg to duration might be extended to include other properties of sound. The most important of these other properties are timbre and dynamic intensity. It took Messiaen seven years, however, to translate these strictly speculative ideas into reality.

Between 1949 and 1950 he wrote the *Quatre études de rythme* for piano. One of the pieces, entitled *Mode de valeurs et d'intensités*, is strictly constructed from the following material:

1 Melodic series of 36 notes
2 Rhythmic series of 24 durations
3 Dynamic series of 7 intensities
4 Timbre series of 7 modes of attack.

Each of the 36 notes of the melodic series has an unchanging duration, intensity and mode of attack. This four-fold determination is then set in three-part canon.

Messiaen's procedure here is different from that of the *Liturgie de cristal* in the *Quatuor*. In the earlier work he had carried out mechanical combinations of 17 rhythms and 29 chords such that each chord could in theory be set against each of 17 different durations. In *Mode de valeurs et d'intensités* the pitch-duration conjunctions are constant, though there are twelve fewer durations than pitches. The *Liturgie de cristal* is comparable in this respect to the Petrarch Sonnet in Schoenberg's *Serenade*, where twelve melody notes are coupled with the eleven-syllable lines of the sonnet, so that one note is left over each time.

In 1952 Messiaen worked for a time at Pierre Schaeffer's Club d'essai and was impressed by the scope and techniques of *musique concrète*. He devised a piece called *Timbres-Durées* which he has said contains no musical sounds. Instead noises are manipulated in various ways: drops of water, jets of water, fountains, high and low cymbals, wood-blocks, snare drum and so forth. These 'timbre-durations' are organised rhythmically (partly in accordance with Indian *tala* models) and are also strictly determined dynamically. The 'parameter' that completely disappears is that of pitch – the very one, in other words, that was the most important in traditional music, as well as in Messiaen's own earlier serial experiments.

It was from these works and experiments of Messiaen that serial composition proper, employing electronic as well as instrumental and vocal techniques, developed. The Darmstadt school, which was chiefly responsible for the spread of serialism and for establishing its claim to an all-inclusive character, is discussed in the next chapter. In France Messiaen's ideas were given a particularly radical twist by a composer who was to employ far more complex mathematical methods: Yannis Xenakis.

Xenakis was born in Athens in 1922 and at first studied architecture. He went to Paris in 1947 and for twelve years was an assistant to Le Corbusier. In 1949 he began to study composition with Honegger and Milhaud, and between 1950 and 1953 he attended Messiaen's rhythm class at the Conservatoire. In July 1955 Hermann Scherchen published an essay by Xenakis in the first volume of the *Gravesaner Blätter* entitled *La crise de la musique sérielle*.

In the article Xenakis claims that two factors have led to the break-up of serial technique: first, linear thinking and the dodecaphonic constraint on which it is based; and secondly, linear polyphony, whose increasing density ('complexité') contains the seed of its own destruction. The effect of dense polyphony on the ear is of an irrational and fortuitous distribution of notes over the sound spectrum; the combinational interchange of twelve notes, although a universal feature of the serial principle, in fact vitiates it.

Xenakis is clearly thinking in terms of something similar to the way in which specks of colour in neo-impressionist paintings should be seen, and make sense, only on the macroscopic level, for he maintains that modern complex linear polyphony collapses into a series of 'statistical' audio-mosaics, as far as the ear is concerned. This being so, he says, the appropriate compositional technique should be provided, not by arithmetic or geometry, but by the calculus of probabilities.

He rejects Messiaen's theory that music can be only an abstract product of thought. 'In this case' he says, 'it is surely nothing but a kind of inductive or deductive logic, a kind of abstract system or philosophy of art. The hypothesis of non-materialised art is a piece of absurd sophistry.'

As a counter-example to the 'linear category' of modern serial composition Xenakis cites three works by Varèse in which agglomerations of rhythms, timbres and dynamic intensities are used: *Intégrales*, *Ionisation* and *Deserts*.

Finally, he adduces various biological facts to show that human beings react to music as to a type of information or communication; indeed, he claims that the modern popularity of jazz is the effect of a double reaction against light music of the folk-song type on the one hand and abstract music on the other.

In October 1955 Hans Rosbaud conducted the first performance of Xenakis's *Metastasis* at Donaueschingen. The piece is written for 63 instruments (mainly strings) and lasts seven minutes. It is built primarily from the string *glissando*. The notation consists of straight lines with defined pitches at their upper and lower limits. The *glissandi* are played simultaneously and produce a 'statistical' effect, a kind of cloud of sound in which no individual note can be distinguished. Xenakis makes a comparison with the sound of the chirping of thousands of cicadas, where no individual insect can be heard but whose overall impression is unambiguous and wholly characteristic: we immediately recognise it as the sound of cicadas. The drumming of heavy rain on a roof is similarly a 'statistical' sound, not a species of polyphony.

Xenakis has steadily continued along this path, advancing by way of *Pithoprakta* (1956) and *Achorripsis* (1956–7) to the colourful succession of electronic and concrete pieces that began with the *Diamorphoses* of 1957. His music, which he calls 'stochastic', gives little inkling of the complicated probability-calculus techniques that it employs. The listener's impression is of a 'global acoustical event', which is as Xenakis wishes. It is immaterial in his view whether a particular note is played or not, since the ear cannot in any case perceive it as a discrete entity. Only the outer limits of the diapason specified for the player in a *glissando* or a multi-tonal cluster have to be observed with painstaking care.

Here then is the paradoxical phenomenon of a musical theory availing itself of higher mathematics, yet stemming from an attitude hostile to geometry. Xenakis, indeed, does not want an art of pure reason, but an art incorporating intuition and emotion. He has also used electronic techniques for his 'stochastic' purposes, most effectively in the short piece *Concret PH* that was produced for the Philips Pavilion at the Brussels Exhibition. Nonetheless, his music is strikingly true to life, sometimes quite disturbingly so. The coolness he early assumed vis-à-vis serial composition comes across to the listener in all his works. At the same time, like the serial composers he attacks, he is fond of launching his works with voluminous commentaries whose cloudy rhetoric confuses rather than enlightens the innocent listener. This also applies to his book *Musiques formelles* (1963): like Schillinger's writings, it is packed with formulae, tables, graphs and drawings of such an esoteric nature that one really needs to be a mathematician in order to penetrate to the meaning of his anti-logical art.

It is noteworthy that Xenakis uses certain arguments similar to those found in conservative writings hostile to non-tonal and twelve-note music. The claim that non-tonal music is 'biologically inferior', for example, had already been put forward in Wilhelm Furtwängler's *Gespräche über Musik* in 1948. It is a corner-stone of Ernest Ansermet's book *Les fondements de la musique dans la conscience humaine* (1961). Both Xenakis and the two great conductors, however, fail to tell us where the line is to be drawn between biological 'feeling' and abstract 'thinking'.

The crisis in serial music of which Xenakis speaks and which is symbolised by his own 'stochastic' music arises from the fact that the new ranges of sound that have been opened up are too extensive to be surveyed. As early as 1920 Hauer, with a mixture of awe and satisfaction, gave the formula for the number of possible combinations of twelve notes: 12! or 479,001,600. It was Ernst Křenek who introduced in 1955 the concept of 'totally pre-determined music'. By this he meant a method of composition such that each element of musical sound – frequency, duration, intensity, timbre, and if possible even the tonal area or ambitus – is determined according to pre-selected series. We already saw in the case of Messiaen's *Liturgie de cristal* that the relatively simple procedure of combining 17 durations with 29 chords leads to a total of possible permutations which is scarcely conceivable, and so to a considerable inflation of form. Clearly, by adding two more series for intensity and timbre we should get a movement of truly mammoth proportions. The composer who prepares his material mathematically beforehand deprives himself of the possibility of generally reviewing and thus fully controlling his material. An electronic computer could of course work out all the possible combinations of the four series, but a composer has necessarily to make a selection from the gigantic sum of possibilities, and this selection will as before have to depend solely on his own subjective disposition. Total pre-determination, in other words, leads directly to a new irrationalism: the mathematical theorist's pipe-dream of ultra-precision is fulfilled only in irrationality.

This is where chance has to take over from precision. We are all familiar with the mathematician's picture of a gigantic library of books containing all possible combinations of letters. The library has whole volumes filled with nothing but the letters a, b, . . . y, z, repeated singly ad infinitum or grouped in meaningless combinations; it also contains the works of Goethe and Shakespeare, Dante and Molière. If we were to select books from this super-library completely at random, our choice would presumably be unsatisfying as literature. Chance undoubtedly plays a part in artistic creation; one of the greatest student of history, Theodor Mommsen, estimated that chance similarly accounts for a third of all historical effects. Yet a view of art in which feeling and intuition take pride of place has little trouble in coming to terms with the caprices of chance. A theory which believes in mathematics and physics as if they were a religion must insure itself against chance's unpredictability and un-reasonableness.

This conflict between the simultaneous pull of determinist calculation and chance is not the monopoly of music today. Modern science has also come to a point where it must invoke a mathematical concept of uncertainty. Heisenberg's indeterminacy relation asserts that a particle's momentum and its location cannot both be precisely determined simultaneously. Admittedly the language of quantum mechanics has been carried over into aesthetic theory in a purely superficial manner, and has been lumped together with mystical and philosophical notions into the bargain. But the general principle holds that mere mathematical devices in the field of art can lead only to a dead end.

Schillinger's attempt to turn art into technology was praise-worthy in inception, but it dangerously under-estimated the irrationality of the creative process. The case of the Bach F major Invention should have been a warning to those who thought that the future of art lay in full-scale rationalisation.

We should not discount the value of intellect in music, any more than we should that of pure imagination. Scientific diagrams and graphs have been used in art for thousands of years. But what of the shapes of clouds, the countless variants of minute biological structures, or the non-calculable factor in the reactions of the sense-organs, even the organs of the artefacts of cybernetics? The old story of the centipede which broke down on being asked how it knew what its twelfth and fifty-eigth feet were doing is relevant to artistic creation.

Every period in the history of art is a demonstration of the Hegelian law of the dialectic. This law says that contradictions can be resolved by syntheses. More exactly, it says that any given phase of development contains within it the elements of the contradictory development: thesis embodies antithesis. In the next phase the elements of the contradictory detach themselves and become independent: the anti-thesis prevails. The forces of the thesis, however, continue to operate imperceptibly until in the next phase, the synthesis, the contradiction is suddenly resolved. This picture is the key to all the apparent contradictions of contemporary music. Just as early in the century the state of freedom gave birth to new means of organisation, so thirty or forty years later these very means of organisation have begun to break up under the impact of quite new demands for freedom.

11 Years of experiment

The Darmstadt Ferienkurse gave a new direction to composition between 1946 and 1955. The courses sprang from the need to release German composers from the twelve-year isolation imposed on them by Nazi *Kulturpolitik*. As part of their artistic 're-education' the composers needed to get to know the works and techniques that had grown up in the years from 1933 to 1945, particularly in the United States. After some cautious early efforts in 1946, mostly under the aegis of neo-classicism *à la* Stravinsky or Hindemith, the second summer saw a growth of interest in the music of the Schoenberg school. The 1948 course was decisive: René Leibowitz attended, a composer and teacher who had studied under Webern and already had been a great influence on the younger generation in France as an advocate of Schoenbergian twelve-note technique. Hans Werner Henze, who had caused a stir at Darmstadt in 1946, and Henze's then teacher Wolfgang Fortner, came to dodecaphony through Leibowitz. Schoenberg was expected to attend in 1949 but was prevented by illness. Messiaen came, however, and it was in Darmstadt that his first serial work *Mode de valeurs et d'intensités* was composed. The way was now clear for the development of the new techniques of composition. In the two following years Varèse, Křenek and leading figures in electronic music and *musique concrète* came to Darmstadt. Varèse's *Ionisation* was given its German premiere under Hermann Scherchen in a sensational programme that also included Fortner's ballet suite *Die weisse Rose*, Schoenberg's *A Survivor from Warsaw*, a *Zwölftonspiel* by Hauer and Křenek's Fourth Symphony.

The first big discussions of serial music were in 1952, when works by Boulez and Stockhausen employing new forms of organisation were performed. Boulez, born in 1925, had studied at the Conservatoire under Messiaen, and between 1945 and 1946 had also worked under Andrée Vaurabourg-Honegger and Leibowitz. Jean-Louis Barrault made him the musical director of his theatre company and under his lead the Théâtre Marigny became an important centre for modern orchestral and chamber music. As early as 1949 his subsequent biographer Antoine Goléa drew attention to his outstanding gifts in an article in the Berlin journal *Stimmen*. Boulez has said that his greatest influences have been Debussy, Stravinsky and Webern, and his most important teacher Messiaen. *Polyphonie X* for seventeen solo instruments was performed in Donaueschingen in 1951, and parts of *Le Soleil des eaux* (with poems by René Char) were heard at the Salzburg ISCM Festival in 1952. In Darmstadt Boulez emerged as a leading advocate of serial and pointillistic techniques, using them in his Second Piano Sonata (1948), *Polyphonie X* and the *Structures* for two pianos (1952–6), which can be regarded as their most thorough-going application. The impression made by all these works, even on a listener who had read the commentaries beforehand, was one of chaos. They put one in mind of multi-coloured oscillograms in which the traditional categories of melody and harmony had been suppressed in favour of shock effects of dynamics and timbre. The fact that these shock effects were organised according to pre-chosen series was only of theoretical interest.

After 1954 Boulez took up an aesthetic position midway between Debussy and his idol Webern. He was also the source of a general coolness towards Schoenberg, whom he respected as the great inspirer and creator of twelve-note technique but still ranked lower than Webern. Boulez's unusual musical language was made most clearly manifest in 1955, with the performance of his vocal and instrumental cycle *Le Marteau sans maître* at the Baden-Baden ISCM Festival, which sparked off bitter arguments and sharply divided listeners into two camps of admirers and detractors. The work, which has been considerably revised, is a *concertante* setting of three surrealist poems by René Char for solo contralto and a chamber ensemble. Four of the nine movements in the final version are vocal, five purely instrumental. One of the poems appears in two different settings.

The chirping, knocking, porcelain-like sounds of *Le Marteau*, as always in Boulez, have an aura of inspired unpredictability that is strangely at odds with the mathematical determinism of the work's serial construction. It is scored for alto flute, guitar and viola, and the contrasting, unusual timbres of xylophone and vibraphone. The whimper of the vibraphone pervades the overall sound. The xylo-

Boulez (*b*. 1925).

phone is given a varied, virtuoso-concertante treatment, notably in the middle section of the second movement, *Commentaire I de 'bourreaux de solitude'*. The voice is used with the utmost daring, indulging at one moment in melismatic acrobatics, at the next in great single-syllable leaps: it is vocal writing that clearly derives from Webern and marks an assault on the French tradition of *chanson* and aria. The overall abruptness of style, the pointillistic melodic writing and seemingly arbitrary rhythms are also reminiscent of exotic models. The work contains passages of great beauty and peculiar persuasiveness. Yet, as in Messiaen, certain passages are over-extended and extravagant in a manner that is wholly un-French.

In line with the French tradition of theorising about art, of which he is highly conscious, Boulez has related his ideas and work to various literary exemplars. His models are Mallarmé, Joyce and the diaries of Paul Klee. His theories are speculative, liable at all times to be subjected to self-criticism, stood on their head, or scrapped altogether. 'Schoenberg est mort' is the title of an essay in which he makes a vehement apology for dodecaphony.

However, his strict serial organisation has more recently made way for a new kind of freedom. The outward impression of arbitrariness, the seemingly improvised quality that his music had had even when determined down to the last detail, has become one of its key formal principles, i.e. a property of its internal structure. An almost-forgotten concept has suddenly re-entered contemporary terminology: improvisation. Composition has ceased to be the once-and-for-all unalterable determination of musical elements; instead the music is to be created *ad hoc*, in and through the act of performance.

Boulez's Third Piano Sonata was written in 1957. It is a work similar in structure to Stockhausen's much-discussed experimental piece *Klavierstück XI* (1956), but conceived on a larger scale. Both works show the influence of John Cage, who had been using chance methods since 1951, e.g. in his *Music for Piano 1*. All three composers were also influenced by non-European techniques: Boulez and Stockhausen had studied classical Indian *ragas* and *talas* under Messiaen and had thus become familiar with a highly flexible type of *ad hoc* composition in which at least two elements, melodic and rhythmic, are given in advance.

We saw in chapter 10 how Xenakis's stochastic music was reaction against an arithmetical and geometrical mentality. John Cage came to substantially similar results by a quite different route. Cage was born in Los Angeles in 1912, where he studied composition with Henry Cowell and Adolphe Weiss and piano with Richard Buhlig. He also attended Schoenberg's classes at the University of California at Los Angeles. After a period in teaching and administration he moved to New York. In 1938 he introduced the 'prepared piano', a piano with pieces of metal, rubber and other materials fitted between the strings, and for it he wrote a large number of pieces, beginning with a *Bacchanal* (1938) for the dancer Syvilla Fort. 'The need to change the sound of the instrument arose through the desire to make an accompaniment, without employing percussion instruments', Cage has written. In the *Sonatas and Interludes*, performed at Columbia University in 1949, the piano sound is made to resemble a wide variety of noises. Cage had already experimented with note-repetitions, rhythmic models, proportional forms and fragmentary note-series.

Since 1951 he has produced compositions which may be characterised as follows:

1 Works involving chance operations;
2 works using template stencils;
3 works based on imperfections in the manuscript paper;
4 works in which the voice has no fixed relation to the score;
5 works whose performance is indeterminate.

Cage's ideas embrace the Chinese chance technique of coin throwing from the *I-Ching*, the mysticism of Meister Eckardt, and Zen Buddhism. He has justified his doctrine of 'indeterminacy' by appeal to Bach, pointing out that the instrumentation of *The Art of Fugue* can vary at the performers' discretion and from one occasion to the next.

Underlying all his theorising, however, is an impulse towards dissociation. This does not merely include compositional elements and materials: Cage wishes the artist to be dissociated from society and to become the centre of a kind of cult of the absurd. In this sense Cage's music is an extension of the Dada destructivism of 1916 to 1920. His performances with David Tudor on two pianos (usually prepared pianos) are strange exhibitions indeed. They, too, can be seen as going back to the anti-social practical jokes perpetrated by the Dadaists in the Cabaret Voltaire in Zürich during the First World War. The difference is that what was then a form of scornful protest against the world's self-destruction has now become little more than a negative art for art's sake.

In October 1954 Cage and Tudor appeared at the Donaueschingen Festival. The outcome of their performance, and of some tapes that were played, was a number of new sound materials, mostly of a bizarre kind. One of the pieces that was given its premiere was called *12' 55.677 for Two Pianists*. It lasted for about thirteen minutes of chirping, drumming sounds, mostly ejected as explosive staccatos. Occasionally Tudor got hold of a whistle or a toy trumpet and blew cat-calls. Then he began to bang on some metal with a hammer. Eventually he crawled under his piano to make running repairs, leaving Cage to play on undisturbed. Another Cage piece performed at Donaueschingen was called *Williams Mix*. The pianos were not used; instead eight tape recorders were relayed over eight loudspeakers distributed around the hall. In later concerts (since 1958) Cage has used several radios playing simultaneously while tuned to different local stations. This took the doctrine of chance to limits and removed the last traces of control by guiding creator.

Cage's methods (extended to the voice in the *Aria* of 1958) have been influential. His experiments with chance and his cult of the absurd and the grotesque have inspired a special genre of avant-garde musical cabaret which has spread to the concert hall and the theatre. Some of these highbrow musical ventures have had affinities with developments in popular music such as rock 'n' roll.

Boulez's reaction to Cage was both productive (viz. the Third

Cage (b. 1912) introduced the concept of 'indeterminacy' into modern music (Zen Buddhism may lie behind this preoccupation with chance factors). Many of his works are for the 'prepared piano' and its distorted sounds, and Cage uses Dadaist, a-logical ideas both in his theoretical and his musical offerings. He is a prolific and stimulating man of great influence, though in which direction this influence will finally be seen to have operated most effectively cannot be guessed at.

Piano Sonata) and polemical. His essay *Alea*, published in the 1958 *Darmstädter Beiträge* speaks, with clear reference to Cage, of the

adoption of a philosophy tinged with orientalism serving to mask fundamental weaknesses of compositional technique.

However, Boulez attacks no less harshly the total serialism of the type he had previously practised himself, accusing it of number fetishism and of being purely mechanistic and automatic. He denounces both methods as

refusals to choose. The new music of chance is just as fetishist, except that choice is now left to the performer instead of to numbers.

He then proceeds, however, to draw a distinction between

chance through inadvertance and chance through automatism.

And he maintains:

In my experience it is impossible to forsee every meander and virtuality implicit in the original material.

This would lead to irrationality from the other side. It is the same conclusion as had been reached by Křenek in his discussion of 'totally pre-determined music' and Xenakis in his critique of serialism. As Boulez puts it:

One grimly tries to master the material, and equally grimly chance keeps its hold, insinuating itself through a thousand loopholes that cannot be caulked.

He then investigates the possibilities of reconciling composition and chance, mentioning in the process the structural 'formants' and spontaneous improvisation of classical Indian music. By way of notions such as 'rubato', 'ad libitum', and 'fermata', which provide the interpreter with a measure of freedom in traditional music, he comes on to various more sophisticated methods of 'absorbing' chance. One such method – Boulez's term is 'aleatoric', from the Latin alea = dice – is embodied in the Third Piano Sonata.

The Sonata consists of five movements: *Antiphonie*, *Trope*, *Constellation*, *Strophe* and *Séquence*. Under certain conditions the movements can be interchanged. The work is a musical counterpart to Mallarmé's attempt in the *Livre* to use words and syllables as musical elements irrespective of their conventional meaning. Mallarmé's aim had been to combine these elements in different ways so that different poems would be produced. In Boulez's Sonata the movements can come in different orders, and each movement is composed of particles which can themselves be interchanged. In other words, there are variations of chronological sequence in performance, plus variations of other kinds. The performer thus becomes a contributor to the eventual configuration of the work. His task may be compared with that of an organist or pianist realising a figured bass, except that the constants and variables are different.

It is evident that aleatoricism entails a break-up of the traditional concept of form. The beginning and end of a composition are not fixed, but can assume several shapes. Laws of construction, intensification and development as worked out in classical tonal music are discarded. Nonetheless, Boulez's Sonata is not governed by blind chance as is the case in Cage, nor by near-blind chance as in

Stockhausen: in Boulez's own phrase, chance is guided. The work roughly resembles a sculpture, which can be seen from different angles, or the mobiles of Alexander Calder. The titles of two of the movements of the Third Sonata, incidentally, *Trope* and *Constellation*, are borrowed from Hauer's writings on twelve-note technique.

In its theoretical assumptions Stockhausen's *Klavierstück XI* falls midway between the irreconcilable standpoints of Cage and Boulez. The former has called it conventional, the latter has censured its 'new automatism'.

Karlheinz Stockhausen (born 1928) was roused by Cage from his mathematical dreams. In 1952 he was an uncompromising advocate of *durchgeordnete Musik*, though by 1954 he was already speaking

Stockhausen (b. 1928) studied in Cologne and attended courses on *musique concrète* and electronic music at the 1951 Darmstadt summer school. He was influenced by Messiaen and Schaeffer, to whose Paris studio for 'phono-montages' he was an early visitor. Thereafter he worked on electronic music, and since 1963 has directed the electronic studio at Cologne Radio.

in terms of 'statistical form' and 'approximate determination'. In the wind quintet *Zeitmasse* he attempted to compose indeterminacy relationships by combining measured time with subjectively experiential time. The *Klavierstück XI* was written in 1956 and published by Universal Edition of Vienna on a large rectangular sheet 21 by 36 inches. The score consists of nineteen note groups in normal notation distributed unevenly over the page. (Cage: 'The only unconventionality is its format'). The playing instructions are as follows:

> The performer looks at random at the sheet of music and begins with any group, the first that catches his eye; this he plays, choosing for himself tempo (small notes always excepted), dynamic level and type of attack. At the end of the first group, he reads the tempo, dynamic and attack indications that follow, and looks at random to any other group, which he then plays in accordance with the latter indications. . . . Each group can be joined to any of the other 18: each can thus be played at any of the six tempi and dynamic levels and with any of the six types of attack. . . . This Piano Piece should if possible be performed twice or more in the course of a programme.

When a note-group is repeated, Stockhausen specifies variants, e.g. octave displacements, additional or omitted notes, and so forth.

In 1960 the little pieces of dramatic business *à la* Dada which had been in vogue at avant-garde concerts were expanded into theatrical performances. Modern music teamed up with the theatre of the absurd of Beckett and Ionesco. John Cage put on his *Theater Piece 1960* at the Circle on the Square Theatre in New York. The performers were himself and David Tudor, a contralto, a tuba player, and the dancers Merce Cunningham and Carolyn Brown. The piece was based on a scheme of simultaneous incoherent actions and 'happenings'. The performers shot at balloons filled with paint; one of them had a shave while the March from *Tannhäuser* issued from a loudspeaker and the contralto sang Lucienne Boyer's twenties hit *Parlez-moi d'amour*. Cage's role was restricted to standing in a corner of the little arena and counting very slowly from one to twenty-three. The whole affair was cheerful rather than outrageous, rather like a circus taken over by the clowns.

Soon afterwards Stockhausen put on a piece called *Originale* at a small theatre in Cologne (first performance: 26 October 1961). The main principles were the same as in Cage's piece, namely simultaneity and systematised clowning. The musical part of the performance was Stockhausen's composition No. 12, *Kontakte* (1960), for electronic sounds, piano and percussion. The players were David Tudor and the percussionist Christoph Kaskel. The performing directions for *Originale* have been published. Scene 14B runs:

> Pianist and percussionist put on clothes brought in by the cloakroom attendant. The pianist takes off his cultic robes and puts on Oriental female costume. . . . When he is ready, he begins to brew up tea at the piano.

The German-Argentinian composer Mauricio Kagel (born 1931) has also contributed to this musical theatre of the absurd. He attended Darmstadt in 1958, proving himself with a string sextet as a highly capable and well-trained *espressivo* composer. His chamber-music theatre piece in one act *Sur scène* was first performed in Bremen in 1962. The work is a piece of didactic cabaret, with music cut down to the minimum. Various items of action unfold simultaneously, sometimes joining together. A professor of music delivers polemical lectures; someone mimes *à la* Marcel Marceau; a singer clears his throat and begins to sing, making menacing gestures; three performers start practising the piano, harmonium, celesta and an assortment of percussion.

The height of absurdity was reached when a Korean called Nam Yune Pak staged revivals of old Dada routines. It is understandable that many modern composers, finding composition impossible, should turn to grotesque jokes and 'happenings'. Fun and games, however, do not compensate for diminishing musical returns. Boredom soon sets in and the listener finds himself craving for the inspired nonsense of an old Marx Brothers film.

The attempts that have been made to achieve formal syntheses of language and music have been much more serious. Boulez in particular has carried out important work here in his Mallarmé cantatas, which began as *Improvisations sur Mallarmé* in 1958 and have provisionally ended as *Pli selon pli*. Several composers including Stockhausen and Nono have concurrently studied and exploited the phonetic and semantic properties of the spoken syllable. Fritz Winckel and other scientists have made both joint and individual contributions to this research. Words have become a weapon in the musical armoury: singers are required to produce all kinds of timbres from sung notes to whispers, hisses and the like. In respect of both technique and theory all these experiments go back to Schoenberg's *Pierrot Lunaire*. The later sound-montages of the Dadaists have also been a source of material. In 1928 the Czech composer Emil Burian demonstrated his 'Voice-band' at the ISCM festival in Siena, which was able to create vivid effects by using innumerable modifications of the sung and spoken voice, rhythmically organised noises and imitations of animals. Burian later also used these methods in the theatre in Prague, particularly for the political stage after 1937. From the literary point of view, the sources of inspiration for this work in the no-man's-land between music and literature have been the writings of James Joyce and August Stramm, and for a short while also the 'lettrisme' of Isidore Isou. The model for Wladimir Vogel's *Arpiade* of 1958 was the lyric poetry of Jean Arp. It is a setting of eight surrealist poems for an ensemble of mixed speech-chorus, soprano and various instruments. Its combination of sensitive, variegated sound, rhythm and melody with a text that ingeniously exploits the findings of depth psychology, suggests new possibilities.

In Italy the chief exponents of this type of speech-composition have been Luigi Nono, who dismembers the texts of his highly artistic settings of poems in a manner that makes them incomprehensible to the listener, and Luciano Berio (born 1925). Berio's works for the singer Cathy Berberian, notably *Esposizione*, which made a fascinating impression when performed in a stage version by Ann Halprin and the Dancer's Workshop in Venice in 1963, have given new dimensions to the theatre of the absurd.

In 1956 the dodecaphonic and serial techniques of the younger generation found support from a wholly unexpected quarter:

Stravinsky. Stravinsky had already used serial shapes (*Grundgestalten*), canonic imitation and mirror forms in the *Cantata* (1952), the Shakespeare songs (1953) and the canons *In Memoriam Dylan Thomas* (1954). The Septet for three wind instruments, three strings and piano (1953) had clearly betrayed the influence of Schoenberg and Webern. Since the *Canticum Sacrum* (1956) he has written twelve-note music. Indeed, in the *Movements* for piano and orchestra, having defended the rights of tonality so long and so passionately, he abandons tonal ties altogether.

This latter-day conversion was as bewildering, and as much of a shock for his supporters, as his conversion to neo-classicism in 1920. The fact that it was made manifest in major religious works, the *Canticum Sacrum*, *Threni* (1958) *A Sermon, a Narrative and a Prayer* (1962) and *The Flood* (1963), only invested it with additional authority. Between 1954 and 1957 came the ballet *Agon*, which is based at one and the same time on traditional French dance forms, canonic and fugal techniques, and note-series that are partly dodecaphonic.

Stravinsky has undergone several striking conversions as a composer: from a Russian late-romantic with leanings towards folk music, to a French classicist, and thence to a supporter of Schoenberg and Webern. Since 1957 he has held his famous *Conversations* with his friend Robert Craft, who has consciously guided and influenced him through this last conversion. To Craft's question: 'What piece of music has most attracted you from a composer of the younger generation?' Stravinsky replied: '*Le Marteau sans maître* by Pierre Boulez'.

Other composers' reactions to the new techniques have been very different. Hindemith flatly dismissed the claims of the much-discussed followers of Schoenberg and Webern in Europe and America. He stuck to the standpoint he had taken up in *Unterweisung im Tonsatz*, where he saw the loss of tonality as a danger to music. At the same time, however, by conducting works by the composers of the Viennese school he evidently drew a distinction between the masters Schoenberg, Berg and Webern and the young post-1945

Berio (b. 1925) uses speech-composition methods to extend the theatre of the absurd into music. The effect is somewhat like that of concrete poetry in reverse.

composers claiming to be their heirs. Benjamin Britten's attitude has been similar. He admires Schoenberg and Berg (with whom he might once have studied) and has used twelve-note themes in *The Turn of the Screw* (1954) and *A Midsummer-Night's Dream* (1961), but he rejects as dangerous 'pressure groups which demand true proletarian music, snobs who demand the latest avant-garde tricks; critics who are already trying to document today for tomorrow' (from the speech *On Receiving the First Aspen Award* in 1964).

On the other hand, there have been signs since 1955 that modern techniques have been influencing young composers in communist countries. In the eyes of official communist cultural policy, of course, all non-tonal music is formalist, Western and decadent, but this has not prevented some gifted and independent-minded composers in various parts of the Soviet Union from studying twelve-note scores. In Moscow Philip Hershkovitz, a pupil of Webern's, has kept up a kind of oral twelve-note tradition. Andrei Volkonsky and possibly others (e.g. Edison Denisov) have received guidance from him. Both composers have brought out dodecaphonic works since 1960:

Volkonsky a cantata based on poems by Lorca, Denisov a set of piano variations.

There is further a group in Kiev which has concerned itself with the music of the Schoenberg school. Konstantin Silvestrov has become known in western Europe for chamber music for various ensembles, including a twelve-note *Trio* for flute, trumpet and celesta (1962). There is also a group in Tallinn, the capital of Estonia, whose reputed head is the conservatoire professor Heino Eller. One of his pupils, Arvo Pärt, has written twelve-note compositions of great brilliance and lucid design, notably a *Perpetuum Mobile* for orchestra.

At the Moscow Summer Music Festival in 1966 discussions were held between composers of differing generations and standpoints. Various speakers wittily disarmed certain prejudices, as the Estonian composer Jan Raetz, who declared: 'Twelve-note technique has as little to do with bourgeois ideology as a double bass'.

One of the greatest problems in using new sound materials is that of notation. How are the unheard-of sounds of *musique concrète* or electronic music, the *glissandi* of Xenakis, or all the nuances of the spoken voice to be notated? Diagrammatic notation of the sort introduced by Schillinger and adopted by Pierre Schaeffer and Stockhausen has not met all needs.

The impossibility of finding an unambiguous notation for certain conceived or conceivable sounds has induced a kind of resignation in some composers. They have made a virtue of necessity and have taken to using pictures as a means of suggestion or a guide for the performer. A work is to be created by improvisation; the performer has to let a scheme of lines, curves and hieroglyphics serve as the stimulus to his imagination. This so-called 'musical graphic', developed particularly by Sylvano Bussotti and realised by the pianist David Tudor, is, in the words of György Ligeti, 'a means, not of communication but of association'. The inventor of these latter-day neumes was once again John Cage; his *Aria* for Cathy Berberian (1958) is notated in the form of a multi-coloured curve that leaves full play to the singer's imagination.

The supplanting of the ear by the eye in musical graphic illustrates a trend that can be observed in various other fields. According to the 'psycho-visualism' of Russel Atkins the hierarchy of the senses is such that the ear is quite incapable of recognising, let alone creating, artistic forms.

Atkins draws a sharp line between music and composition; he claims in fact that they are contradictories. So-called 'musical composition' is a visual art. The ear may be able to distinguish frequencies but it cannot recognise height or depth, structural organisation or geometric relations.

'Eye music', or the use of compositional techniques which the ear cannot (or cannot immediately) register, is nothing new. From the canons of Netherlands Renaissance polyphony to the time of J. S. Bach the composer's eye was always an adjunct of his ear.

Serial music often consciously goes beyond what can be taken in by the ear. It is a disquieting fact that some composers, even such an important composer as Ernst Křenek, have said that it is immaterial whether everything in a composition can be heard or not. This is to cut off music by the very roots.

(It is worth noting that the music of chance, aleatoric music, also has precursors in earlier periods. Johann Philipp Kirnberg's *Methode, Sonaten aus'm Ermel zu schütteln* (1783) and the 'Dice' minuet ascribed to Mozart admittedly use the classical vocabulary, but their game-playing is sublimated into a romantic revolt against the whole notion of fixed and immutable form. We must presuppose a similar underlying attitude in the case of Stockhausen, Boulez and their comrades if their musical kaleidoscopes are to have any sense at all.)

Apart from the synaesthetic art calling itself musical graphic, there have been various other efforts to work out a practical system of notation. A special congress at the Darmstadt Ferienkurse in 1964 was devoted to the problem. Papers were given by the composers Earle Brown (born 1926), Roman Haubenstock-Ramati (born 1919), Mauricio Kagel, György Ligeti (born 1923), the percussionist Christoph Kaskel, the pianist Aloys Kontarsky, the

A page from Cage's *Aria*. The composer's instructions (abridged) read:
The notation represents time horizontally, pitch vertically, roughly suggested . . .
The material, when composed, was considered sufficient for a ten minute
performance (page equals 30 seconds) . . . The vocal lines are drawn in black . . . or
in one or more of eight colours. These differences represent ten styles of singing.
Any ten styles may be used and any correspondence between colour and style may
be established. The one used by Miss Berberian is: dark blue equals jazz; red equals
contralto (and contralto lyric); . . . black equals dramatic; purple equals Marlene

Dietrich; yellow equals coloratura (and coloratura lyric); green equals folk; orange equals oriental; light blue equals baby; brown equals nasal. The black squares are any noises . . . The ones chosen by Miss Berberian . . . are: tsk, tsk; footstomp; bird roll; snap snap (fingers); clap; bark (dog); pained inhalation; peaceful exhalation; hoot of disdain; tongue click; exclamation of disgust; of anger; scream (having seen a mouse); ugh (as suggesting an American Indian); haha (laughter); expression of sexual pleasure. The text employs vowels and consonants and words from five languages: Armenian, Russian, Italian, French and English.

cellist Siegfried Palm and the musicologist Carl Dahlhaus. Although the speakers were unable to agree on a universally valid system of notation, they did demonstrate that the break-up of traditional notation is inevitable in view of the new techniques of composition. Dahlhaus showed in his summary that part of the reason for the present confusion in notation lies in the growing importance of the single, isolated moment in composition itself. This is an important observation, because it draws attention to the new situation that has arisen in listening. The traditional European notion of 'coherence', which was a basic category of the old classical and romantic forms, has, to use a mathematical term, been dethroned by a notion of 'discrete value'. Certainly, contemporary music is 'coherent', whether that music be serial, aleatoric, or totally indeterminate in the sense of John Cage. But its coherence is of a new and different kind: the isolated moment, i.e. the shortest perceptible impression, now fulfils the function previously performed by larger formal sections such as the working-out section. The first hint of this change was shown in the micro-forms cultivated by Schoenberg in 1910 and most notably by Webern thereafter.

The years of experiment have not given rise to any generally accepted styles or techniques of composition, though there has been a striking degree of conformism within individual schools and movements, often to the suppression of all creative individuality. Certain works have been produced which can however be taken as representative. Besides those of Messiaen, Boulez and Stockhausen mentioned earlier, there have been Giselher Klebe's first symphonic work *Die Zwitschermaschine*, after a painting by Klee (1950); Nono's *Epitaffio per F. Garcia Lorca* for choir, soloists and orchestra (1953), a dramatic tableau uniting strict construction with ecstatic *espressivo*; and a cantata by Fortner, *The Creation* (1955) based on the same text by the Negro author Weldon Johnson that Louis Gruenberg had set in 1926, and combining twelve-note series and rhythmic series in the style of the medieval Ars Nova. Further typical works of these years that may be mentioned are Haubenstock-Ramati's *Blessings* for voice and nine instruments (1954), Henze's

12 Consolidation

Works of art are messages despatched to constantly changing addresses. Until the eighteenth century composers were lucky. They wrote either for the greater glory of God or for the prince by whom they were employed. There was never any doubt as to what kind of music would appeal to pious church-goers or to the palace guests, albeit that now and then the authorities stepped in with little adjustments or admonitions on aesthetic matters. Not only was the artistic message sent, but it arrived, and was seen to arrive. With the growth first of the bourgeois and then of the proletarian public, this situation changed. Potential listeners – the consumers of music – were no longer cast in the same mould nor had the shared interests of a church congregation or a gathering of noblemen. Audiences became increasingly broadly-based and anonymous. However, within the large and constantly expanding general public new sub-audiences began to form. A group of listeners emerged devoted to the classical and romantic repertoire – a group represented in many countries today by the subscribers to symphony concerts. A special public developed for opera, another for choral music (mostly active participants), a somewhat more exclusive one for chamber music. Lastly, audiences for contemporary music grew up in many cities.

The gap between advanced composers and potential listeners, however, had already widened in the years before the First World War. As compositions and styles increasingly deviated from convention and tradition, and as composers pursued ever more single-mindedly some particular principle of style or technique, so the chances of music being comprehended dwindled. The message was still despatched, but it was no longer addressed. At worst it was a bottle thrown into the sea, its destination unknown.

Attempts were soon made to rescue modern music from its esoteric isolation. An important part was of course played by material forms of assistance from outside. Generally speaking the composer's status had been substantially improved by modern copyright law. From the twenties, too, broadcasting had become sufficient of an economic force to provide employment for the exposed, friendless composers of advanced music. After 1945 radio stations became generous commissioners of contemporary music, even though the new works could be broadcast only on special programmes late at night. The generosity of individual patrons was also an important factor, such as the conductor Serge Koussevitzky and the millionairess Elizabeth Sprague Coolidge in the United States, and the conductor Paul Sacher in Switzerland, as well as numerous foundations established by wealthy individuals. State and civic cultural bodies and composition prizes ensured that serious modern music brought composers some material reward, despite a relative dearth of performances. Opera houses and universities commissioned works: as in broadcasting, the composer profited from a general desire to be in with the latest fashion. Yet in spite of all this many composers felt inhibited and oppressed by a lack of well-defined creative, intellectual and spiritual goals.

Some looked for a belief or ideal to fill the place formerly occupied by religion. The most appropriate modern panacea to recommend itself was revolutionary socialism or communism. We saw in an earlier chapter how pervasive a phenomenon left-wing 'committed' art was in the twenties and thirties and during the Second World War.

The Venetian composer Luigi Nono was one of the first post-war avant-garde composers to go the way of commitment. A renegade from the classical doctrines of his compatriot Malipiero, Nono was led by Hermann Scherchen at one and the same time to socialism and to Schoenbergian twelve-note technique. Soon after the *Variazioni canoniche* on a twelve-note theme of Schoenberg, which enjoyed a *succès de scandale* in Darmstadt in 1950, Nono began to produce political vocal works. The three-movement Lorca epitaph previously mentioned falls in this category, particularly the third movement, which uses *Sprechstimme* and speech chorus. Speech-choruses also play an important part in the later work *La victoire de Guernica* (1954). *Il Canto Sospeso*, based on letters of Resistance fighters written before execution, is the first summit in Nono's committed output. It is scored for three solo voices, mixed choir and orchestra, and as a musical realisation of the tragic words it has a dramatic impact that sweeps aside all the structural complexities of the score. His next major landmark, reached by way of the *Cori di Didone* for choir and percussion of 1958 (based on poems by Guiseppe Ungaretti) and smaller choral pieces, was the opera *Intolleranza* (1960), which made a strong impression on audiences when it was performed in Venice and Cologne. To be sure, there were also political demonstrations bordering on riots when the opera – or *azione scenica*, as Nono has termed it – was performed in Venice, and the prolonged applause it received in Cologne was likewise punctuated by whistling and booing. But these are the inevitable accompaniments of a work so accusatory in character. *Intolleranza* is a political opera, a loosely dramatised protest against inhumanity and the police state. Its eleven scenes have a literary ancestry going back to Büchner, Zola and Gerhart Hauptmann. The libretto uses quotations from Sartre and Brecht, and borrows various techniques from the German inter-war theatre of Ernst Toller and Friedrich Wolf and the drama of Eugene O'Neill and Arthur Miller. The plot is very freely put together and is Nono's own selection from a much more extensive libretto by Angelo Maria Ripellino. The central character is a refugee, a miner, who is driven back to his native land by homesickness. His flight separates him from his wife, who becomes his enemy. He gets unwittingly caught up in a political uprising, which involves him in brain-washing, torture and the horrors of a concentration camp, but also teaches him the meaning of solidarity, friendship and love. At the close of the opera, almost as in *Götterdämmerung*, the earth is engulfed by a flood, but the belief that the world can be changed survives. The opera ends with a chorus from Brecht's *An die Nachgeborenen*.

A work of this kind, clearly directed against fascist dictatorship, makes demands on the tolerance of liberals if it is to be publicly performed. Committed to the left as it is, it makes no mention of the Stalinist inhumanity with which the uprisings in Leipzig and Budapest were put down, nor the shooting of dissenters who attempt to cross the Iron Curtain.

Nono dedicated the opera to Schoenberg. Perhaps he wished

Nono (b. 1924). His message is simpler than his music.

thereby to signal the fact that a composer's commitment can be justified only by the highest art. The work is written in a difficult musical language and calls for a very complicated battery of sound-sources: an orchestra of eighty, a large mixed chorus, five soloists and several speakers. The choruses are recorded on tape and transmitted to the audience over several channels so that a formal effect of circular movement is produced.

The writing has the expressive density and strangely fluctuating, sharply-focused luminosity of sound that Nono showed earlier. Wind and percussion timbres are distorted by the use of *Flatter-zunge*, tremolo and many *ad hoc* techniques. As always in Nono, the work's inspiration, intellectual integrity and complete rigour are unquestionable. Its agglomerations of extremes of sound and its un-inhibited use of new materials are typical of a first attempt at a new form. As a step on the way to a mastery of the operatic medium it has key significance for the composer. *Intolleranza* has a solitary position in contemporary music: it is a species of topical music-cum-theatre that has not existed since the twenties and thirties.

In the *Canciones a Guiomar* (1962–3) for soprano, female chorus and small instrumental ensemble, based on texts by Antonio Machado, Nono has created a small masterpiece. The cantata is a fragment of life itself, brimming with new sonorities, which re-echo in a tissue of sound in the postlude for four groups of six female voices. Nono's intellectual situation is paradoxical. He lives in Italy, under the capitalism and democracy he rejects. The music he writes is viewed with disfavour in the Soviet Union, where he has offered samples of it; it is too advanced even within the somewhat more tolerant atmosphere of post-Stalinist cultural policy. Only the future will show whether the blend of revolutionary conviction and musical modernism that Nono advocates has a chance of survival.

Some composers in communist countries have followed a path that must be regarded as strangely at odds with Nono's art of commitment. In Poland, where there has been tolerance in the arts since the 1956 uprising, modern techniques and styles of composition have become amazingly widespread. The Warsaw Festivals which have been held every autumn since 1957 have made available for discussion a wide range of works from many countries. Works by the rearguard of 'socialist realists' have rubbed shoulders with Western experimental compositions. Here is a breakdown of the works performed at one festival (1962): twenty-one works by dead composers (including Bartók, Berg, Debussy, Janáček, Malawski, Martinu, Pijper, Prokofiev, Schoenberg, Szymanowski and Webern), twenty by living Polish composers, seven by Stravinsky, seven from Italy, six from West Germany (counting Hindemith), five from the Soviet Union, four from the United States, three from Britain, two from Czechoslovakia and one each from Argentina, Belgium, Bulgaria, Greece, Holland, Japan, Rumania, Sweden and Switzerland. Thirteen of these were first performances, of which ten were of Polish works. The majority of these were non-tonal.

Glissandi and tone-clusters were much in evidence in these 1962 Polish works. Wojciech Kilar (born 1932) used them to virtuoso effect in a piece called *Riff 62* for piano and orchestral groups. Harmonics, *tremoli* and alarming wind accents combined to form a structure based on colour rather than contour. The score's great effectiveness was heightened by a big percussion crescendo. The *Chants instrumentaux* by Henryk Gorecki (born 1933) also inhabited the no-man's-land between musical sound and noise. The most vivid colours in this work were *glissandi*, piano clusters, plucked guitar, wood-blocks and trumpet *fortissimi*.

In *Musica ipsa* by Boguslaw Schaeffer (born 1929), the author of important books on contemporary music, howling *glissandi* interrupted by violent outbursts of noise, spoke of a powerful emotional purpose. The twelve-note Second Symphony by Zigmunt Mycielski, and eclectic works such as the *Concerto for Orchestra* by Grazyna Bacewicz (born 1913), *Segmenti* by Kazimierz Serocki (born 1922) and *Variations sans thème* by Tadeusz Baird, impressed by their solidity as well as their non-conformity.

Two composers stood and stand out head and shoulders above the others by virtue of their great gifts and creative individuality: Witold Lutoslawski and Krzystof Penderecki. Lutoslawski was born in 1913, and studied mathematics at the University of Warsaw and piano, violin and composition at the Conservatory. His music written between 1945 and 1954 achieves an integration of Polish folk-music comparable with Bartók's use of Hungarian folk-music. After 1956 he revised his technique of composition, adopting first Schoenbergian twelve-note technique and then by degrees the serial, aleatoric and speech-composition methods of western Europe. He achieved world recognition with the *Funeral Music* for string orchestra (1956–8), which is now in the international orchestral repertoire. The work is in four parts without breaks (*Prologue – Metamorphosis – Apogée – Epilogue*) and is constructed from a twelve-note series of semitones and tritones. It is based on variation and canon and is as close in style to Berg as it is to Bartók, to whose memory it is dedicated. For all the strictness of the construction it is *espressivo* music of the most moving kind, as poignant in its quiet mourning as in its wild outbursts of grief.

Lutoslawski's *Trois poèmes d'Henri Michaux* was the most compelling work performed at the 1963 Zagreb Biennale, which along

with the Warsaw Festival is the chief outlet for modern music in eastern Europe. In the lyrical *Pensées* wind, two pianos, xylophone, harp, celesta and percussion accompany the choir in a sweeping advance from iridescent sounds and dense note-clusters using micro-intervals towards a tempestuous, dramatic eruption. The climax comes in *Le grand combat*, where speech-chorus and a concerto of noises merge into musical sounds, frozen cries and a sudden, shattering *crescendo*. In *Repos dans le malheur* the tensions are released, as soprano and baritone solos dispersed among the choral parts give way to harp, piano and female voices, and the work fades peacefully into silence.

Penderecki (born 1933) first attracted attention as Poland's most advanced experimentalist with sound with his *Anaklasis* (1960) for percussion groups and forty-two strings. The programme note for the work's Donaueschingen premiere was written by the composer himself, and discusses factors of rhythmic organisation (rotation, arithmetical series) and sound-spaces filled by quarter-tones and semi-tones:

Lutoslawski (b. 1913), one of many Polish experimentalists to have benefited from the liberal artistic climate of the post-1956 period. His early works were rooted in Polish folk-music, much as Bartók belongs to the Hungarian popular tradition. Lutoslawski's *Funeral Music* with its Bartók dedication and its echoes of Berg makes a forward link to the composer's adoption of serial, aleatoric and speech-composition methods in more recent works.

The chief principle of organisation (in normal performance) is the division of the instruments into what might be called colour groups and – somewhat as in the concerto grosso – the bringing out of given instruments within some of these groups. The groups are contrasted with one another and the composer has made use of their rich and varied possibilities of articulation. He has used special effects with certain instruments (e.g. prepared piano), and with the strings he has operated on several levels of sound-space, thereby producing colour effects reminiscent of electronic music.

Penderecki's language in the work is anti-polyphonic; his aim is to create noises out of musical sounds. In *Canon* for fifty-two strings, first performed in Warsaw in 1963, he twice confronts the first formal section with a recording of itself on tape, uniting them in canon (including in retrograde). Haubenstock-Ramati had already made a similar experiment in his *Interpolations*. The instruments in *Canon* eschew their conventional sound; they are struck, rubbed, bowed *col legno*, and used almost entirely to produce noises of varying colour. The style is that of Varèse and Xenakis, and Penderecki handles it with a sure sense of contrast, form and coherence, yet also with a steely rigour.

Non-normative and 'absolute' as the Polish applications of modern techniques and means of expression may be, there is at the same time a not easily definable form of higher-order commitment in their work. One is always conscious of a special quality of personal engagement, of underlying intellectual and material insecurity. Chopin's ardent patriotic feeling and Szymanowski's sublimated modern *Weltschmerz* are complemented in Lutoslawski and Penderecki by the ineradicable imprint of the nightmare of 1939–45. To this must be added the emotional impact of the second liberation of 1956 and an innate propensity towards religion. Penderecki's Hiroshima threnody had already identified him as a politically committed composer, but he then went on to bring out the *Psalms of David* (1958) and an unaccompanied *Stabat Mater* that is much sung in Poland. In the same year Cologne Radio commissioned him to write a Passion according to St Luke, which was performed for the first time in Münster Cathedral in 1963. The work is in two parts and lasts over an hour; it calls for three soloists, a speaker, three mixed choirs, boys' choir and orchestra. The score is founded on a twelve-note series incorporating the notes B-A-C-H and uses *glissandi*, quarter-tones, 'statistical' agglomerations of notes and clusters. The chanting, whispering, hisses and mocking laughter of the choruses are reminiscent of the vocal world of Nono, who in all other aspects can be regarded as Penderecki's spiritual and political opposite. With the *St Luke Passion* a member of a communist state has built the most important bridge between religious tradition and the New Music since Stravinsky and Webern. The Passion has been translated into a symbol of humanity.

These Polish composers have set an important example of consolidation in modern music. They have had an effect on the Zagreb school, notably on Milko Kelemen (born 1924), its most active spokesman and representative. Since 1960 the younger generation in Spain has also established contact with central Europe, helped by an almost complete relaxation of domestic restrictions on artistic expression. The most active young Spanish composers have been Luis de Pablo (born 1930) and Cristobal Halffter (born 1930). The turmoil of anguish and fear contained within a lucid formal structure of Halffter's *Espejos* (for four percussionists and tape recorder) remains the outstanding memory of the first Madrid Biennale for modern music of December 1964.

The breakthrough in new ideas and techniques was as explosive an occurrence in Spain as it is in any country where youth feels confined by an anti-modernistic regime and seeks to break out. Change and upheaval are welcome in any nation as evidence of intellectual freedom. Whether they will also release genuine creative forces, as has undoubtedly happened in Poland, depends on factors over and beyond the immediate social and political situation. Every nation has long-run variations in artistic creativity, but the reasons for them have so far eluded the sociologists and psychologists.

There now exist in Barcelona and Madrid various overlapping and conflicting groups who regard themselves, with a measure of rebellious pride, as an avant-garde. They do not mix with the

Penderecki (b. 1933) and the score of his *St Luke Passion*, the most successful bridge between the religious tradition and the New Music since Stravinsky and Webern.

conservative middle-class cultural establishment. The musicians and painters think in cosmopolitan terms and for some time have had links with like-minded groups abroad. Recently they have also had some government support.

The beginning of the period of consolidation in modern music can be fairly precisely dated. In the middle of the fifties the paths of two composers of quite different generations crossed: Stravinsky, nearly seventy, adopted the dodecaphonic and serial techniques he had so long rejected; Hans Werner Henze (born 1926), more than forty years his junior, joined the Stravinskyians and dissociated himself step by step from the advanced compositional techniques which at Darmstadt he had been one of the first to employ.

Even Henze's early works, ranging from chamber music for all kinds of ensembles to ballet, revealed a tendency towards synthesis. After 1947 Henze sought to achieve a combination of dodecaphony, neo-classical forms and Stravinskyian rhythms. The opera *Boulevard Solitude* (1951) includes serial forms of organisation, noise montages, jazz, *Sprechstimme* and sweet vocal cantilenas. In *König*

244

Hirsch formal construction takes second place to a new melodic style influenced by Italian folk-song and *bel canto*. Unlike many musicians, painters and writers of his generation, Henze's problem is not how to fill up an organisational structure but how to organise the fullness of his material.

Like Schoenberg and Berg, Henze allows that certain applications of tonality can be compatible with panchromaticism and twelve-note writing. The magic opera *König Hirsch* was followed by two ballets, the naturalistic *Maratona di Danza* and the neo-romantic *Undine* (1956). Henze's language in these works is not the language of the New Music, but it bears the imprint of the earlier experience, in much the same retrospective fashion as Stravinsky's *Apollon Musagète* and *Le Baiser de la fée* or the mature works of Britten.

The earlier lessons are summarised in *Der Prinz von Homburg*, whose libretto was adapted by Ingeborg Bachmann from Kleist's play. Henze here writes music purely and simply – shaped, moulded to fit the course of the action, informed with emotion yet precisely controlled. The vocal writing subserves the text yet still obeys its own inherent formal laws.

'I have needed all my strength to write simply,' Henze once said in a discussion with students. This does not mean he has given up serialist constructional games. The *Antifone* for orchestra, conducted by Herbert von Karajan in Berlin, and the Piano Sonata are built with all the strict discipline he had learnt from serialism. But in opera he keeps to a more traditional path, the path that had already been indicated by W. H. Auden in his libretto for Stravinsky's *The Rake's Progress*.

The *Elegy for Young Lovers* and *Die Bassariden* (1966) both have libretti by Auden and Chester Kallmann. With them and the buffa opera that came between them, *Der junge Lord*, Henze rounded off a change of style comparable to the self-revisions of Strauss and Hindemith and to Stravinsky's return to classicism between 1919 and 1950. The paradox is that Stravinsky and Henze should have crossed paths at the very moment when their styles were being re-orientated in diametrically opposite directions.

Both re-orientations, however, have been important instances of the process of consolidation within modern music. Stravinsky has used the techniques of the younger generation to write religious works which link up with his earlier music, notably the *Symphony of Psalms* and the Mass. *Agon* is a synthesis of modern and medieval procedures.

Henze in some of his latest works has given expression to humanist ideals. His oratorio *Novae de infinito laudes*, based on writings of Giordano Bruno, is about the rights of man and freedom of thought. Henze informs us that it is 'composed for many voices and a large consort of lutes, pianos, harps, cors anglais, trumpets and trombones'.

Other important composers of our time are similarly committed to a non-political form of humanism. We have already referred to an early work of Benjamin Britten in which he voiced his feelings on the Spanish civil war. His *War Requiem* likewise relates to historical events and is a plea for human reconciliation and pacifism. Humanitarian sympathies are also to be found in Britten's seemingly message-less operas *Peter Grimes*, *The Turn of the Screw* and *Billy Budd*. Britten's art is always sustained by his belief in communication and his awareness of the need for a generally comprehensible language when ideas of general concern are to be expressed. This brings him close to the communist philosophy of art and, by reason of his scepticism towards experiment, makes him a spiritual ally of Shostakovich.

In Italy Luigi Dallapiccola has been the most powerful and persuasive representative of this kind of universal humanism. From the start his work has been at the very centre of the dialogue between freedom and repression. The title of the *Canti di prigionia* and the opera *Il prigioniero* speak for themselves, and similar themes recur in his numerous settings from the Greek, Italian and Spanish. At the same time Dallapiccola has always remained faithful to the advanced techniques developed by Schoenberg and Berg, though he has derived from them a free and highly distinctive style of his own. Among Scandinavian composers Karl-Birger Blomdahl has dealt with contemporary problems in his powerful opera *Aniara* (libretto by Erik Lindegren).

In Germany the whole creative effort of Karl Amadeus Hartmann (1905–63) was dedicated from 1934 onwards to the humanistic ideal of freedom. Hartmann did not leave Germany during the Hitler period, but he maintained an intellectual form of resistance to the regime, with the result that until 1945 his works were only performed abroad. When he went to study with Webern in 1941–2 he already had a number of major works to his credit, including the opera *Simplicius Simplicissimus* (1934–5), which was not performed until 1949 in Cologne. In eight important works he gave the symphonic form new life, (a form which has otherwise been neglected by modern composers outside Russia), extending the formal principles of Mahler yet employing a distinctive and unmistakable musical language of his own that includes twelve-note series and variable metres. His First Symphony (1937), also composed before his period of study with Webern, is called *Versuch eines Requiems* ('Attempt at a Requiem'). The orchestra is joined by a contralto in a setting of the same poem that Hindemith later used in his requiem for the dead of the Second World War, Whitman's 'When lilacs last in the dooryard bloom'd'. The Second Symphony, in a single movement, is a powerful Adagio in the manner of the slow movements of Mahler and Berg. Similar elegaic movements recur in the Fourth Symphony for strings (1947), the Sixth Symphony and the Seventh. The moving pathos of Hartmann's writing, which also informs his string quartets, concertos and cantatas, is one of the most precious offerings of recent German music.

Boris Blacher is Hartmann's complete antithesis. His is an art of anti-romanticism, of studied parsimony of feeling; his musical language has been ruthlessly stripped of every non-essential. Within this *style depouillé* his vocal music and operas have given striking expression to humanitarian ideals. He, too, is concerned with the freedom of the individual; the theme is found in the oratorio *Der Grossinquisitor* (1942) based on the story by Dostoievsky, the chamber opera *Die Flut* (1946), the Requiem for soprano, baritone, mixed choir and orchestra (1948), and the opera *Zwischenfälle bei einer Notlandung* (1966) which incorporates electronic music. Blacher has also written an experimental stage work, *Die abstrakte Oper* (1953), which links up with certain tendencies in modern literature and for which Werner Egk wrote a libretto of senseless combinations of words and syllables. The *Preussisches Märchen* (1949) is a light-hearted piece of social indictment; the opera *Rosamunde Floris* (1960; libretto by Georg Kaiser), on the other hand, uses the figure of a woman who has committed murder for love to raise doubts concerning law and conventional morality.

Blacher was also one of five composers who were brought together for the composition of Jens Gerlach's *Jüdische Chronik* ('Jewish Chronicle') for soloists, choir and orchestra. Despite the differences of creative personality between the five (Blacher, Paul Dessau, Hartmann, Henze, and Rudolf Wagner-Regeny) the effect of musical unity that the score produced when it was first performed was astonishing. It showed that a commitment to the tenets of a critical, accusatory text can have a decisive effect on musical style. The five composers were from both East and West Germany; they hardly came into personal contact during the period of composition. Yet the music they wrote for the *Chronicle* testifies to their shared sense of horror and outrage at inhumanity.

Conviction and protest then, can be means of rapprochement. We saw in the cases of Polish and Spanish music that the absence of freedom may similarly spark off creative forces. The results for art are the same. This is also true of the small number of advanced, non-conformist works that have been published in the Soviet Union and in East Germany.

Few ages have set so many problems of musical form and technique as the twentieth century. The world of unfamiliar sounds opened up within the field of chordal and polyphonic music by the surmounting of tonality is even now almost too vast to be surveyed. It has been enlarged by the addition of a whole new world of auditory phenomena, a world of noises and electronically generated sounds that is now vying for equality of status with the first. Innovations

Chronology

Music	Related arts
1854 Janáček b.	
1862 Debussy b.	
1864 R. Strauss b.	
1874 Schoenberg b.	
1875 Ravel b.	
1876 Falla b.	
1881 Bartók b.	
1882 Wagner: *Parsifal*, Stravinsky b.	
1883 Wagner d., Webern b.	
1884 Mahler: *Lieder eines fahrenden Gesellen*	
1885 Bruckner: Eighth Symphony Berg b.	Nietzsche: *Also sprach Zarathustra*
1886 Liszt d.	Seurat: 'La Grande Jatte'
1887 Debussy visits Bayreuth	
1888 Strauss: *Macbeth* Mahler: First Symphony Rimsky-Korsakov: *Sheherazade*	Gauguin: *cloisonnisme*
1889 Strauss: *Don Juan*	Nietzsche becomes insane
1890 Strauss: *Tod und Verklärung*	Van Gogh d.
1891 Prokofiev b.	
1892 Debussy: *Prélude à l'après-midi d'un faune* Milhaud b., Honegger b.	Ibsen: *The Master Builder* Maeterlinck: *Pelléas et Mélisande*
1894 Strauss: *Guntram* Mahler: Second Symphony	Rodin: 'La Pensée'
1895 Strauss: *Till Eulenspiegel* Mahler: Third Symphony	Large Cézanne exhibition at Vollard Gallery
1896 Strauss: *Also sprach Zarathustra*	Verlaine d.
1897 Mahler becomes conductor and director of Vienna Hofoper	George: *Das Jahr der Seele* Wedekind: *Erdgeist* Vienna Sezession founded
1898 Strauss: *Ein Heldenleben*	Mallarmé d.
1899 Schoenberg: *Verklärte Nacht*	
1900 Debussy: *Nocturnes* Schoenberg: *Gurrelieder* Mahler: Fourth Symphony Křenek b.	Freud: *The Interpretation of Dreams* Tolstoy: *Resurrection* Nietzsche d.

1901	Strauss: *Feuersnot*	Th. Mann: *Buddenbrooks*
		Chekhov: *Three Sisters*
1902	Mahler: Fifth Symphony	Picasso: Blue Period
	Debussy: *Pelléas et Mélisande*	
1903	Schoenberg: *Pelleas und Melisande*	Wedekind: *Büchse der Pandora*
	Janáček: *Jenufa* completed	Rilke: *Stundenbuch*
	Stravinsky studies with Rimsky-Korsakov	Gauguin d.
1904	Reger: *Schlichte Weisen*	Braque comes to Paris
	Mahler: Sixth Symphony	Chekhov: *The Cherry Orchard*
	Ives: *March 1776*	
	Berg and Webern study with Schoenberg	
	Dallapiccola b.	
1905	Strauss: *Salome*	Les Fauves at Salon
	Mahler: Seventh Symphony	d'Automne (Vlaminck,
	Debussy: *La Mer*	Derain, Matisse, Rouault)
	Bartók's and Kodály's first researches	Picasso: Pink Period
	into folk-music	
	Debussy: *Images* I	
1906	Schoenberg: First Chamber Symphony	Hauptmann: *Und Pippa tanzt*
	Shostakovich b.	Cézanne d., Ibsen d.
1907	Mahler: Eighth Symphony	Picasso: 'Les demoiselles
	Ravel: *Rapsodie espagnole*	d'Avignon'
	Ives: *Central Park in the Dark*	Kokoschka: 'Die träumenden
	Debussy: *Images* II *for piano*	Knaben'
1908	Mahler: *Das Lied von der Erde*	Rilke: *Neue Gedichte*
	Schoenberg: Second String Quartet	Chagall comes to Paris
	Op.10, Lieder Op. 15 ('free atonality')	
	Berg: Piano Sonata	
	Bartók: *Bagatelles*	
	Ravel: *Ma Mère l'Oye, Gaspard de la nuit*	
	Debussy: *Ibéria*	
	Ives: *The Unanswered Question*	
	Messiaen b.	
1909	Strauss: *Elektra*	Braque and Picasso:
	Mahler: Ninth Symphony	Analytical Cubism
	Schoenberg: Three Piano Pieces Op.11,	First Futurist manifesto
	Five Pieces for Orchestra Op. 16,	*Neue Künstlervereinigung*
	Erwartung Op. 17	formed
	Webern: Five Movements for String	First season of Diaghilev
	Quartet Op. 5	ballet at Théâtre du Châtelet
	Ravel: *Daphnis et Chloé*	
	Ives: First Piano Sonata	
	R.H.Stein: outline of quarter-tones	
1910	Schoenberg: Three Pieces for Chamber	Kandinsky: *Über das Geistige ·
	Orchestra (microforms)	in der Kunst*
	Berg: String Quartet	Cubist exhibition at Salon
	Webern: Four Pieces for Violin and Piano	d'Automne
	Debussy: *Préludes* I, meets Stravinsky	Severini: *simultanité*
	Stravinsky: *The Firebird*	

1911	Strauss: *Der Rosenkavalier* Scriabin: *Promethée* Stravinsky: *Petrushka* Bartók: *Duke Bluebeard's Castle* (first performed 1918) Prokofiev: *Sarcasmes* Mahler d.	Th. Mann: *Der Tod in Venedig* First *Blaue Reiter* exhibition Chagall: 'I and the Village' Chirico: 'La nostalgie de l'infini'
1912	Strauss: *Ariadne auf Naxos* Schoenberg: *Pierrot Lunaire*, Harmonielehre Berg: *Altenberg Leider* Op. 4 Busoni: *Sonatina seconda* Debussy: *Images* completed, *Jeux* Cowell: tone-clusters	*Blaue Reiter* catalogue Braque and Picasso: collages Nolde: 'The Life of Christ'
1913	Schoenberg: *Die glückliche Hand* Stravinsky: *Le Sacre du printemps* Debussy: *Préludes* II Webern: Six Bagatelles for String Quartet Op. 9, Five Pieces for Orchestra Op. 10 Russolo: *bruitismo* Britten b.	Rouault: religious subjects Apollinaire: The Cubist Painters
1914	Berg: Three Orchestral Pieces Op. 6, *Wozzeck* started Hauer: twelve-note compositions Stravinsky: *Pribaoutki* Ives: *Three Places in New England* Casella: *Notte di Maggio*	Stefan George: *Der Stern des Bundes*
1915	Strauss: *Die Frau ohne Schatten* (first performed 1919), *Alpensinfonie* Schoenberg: Four Songs with Orchestra Webern: Songs Op. 12 (1915–17) Debussy: *Études*, *En blanc et noir*, Sonata for Cello and Piano Falla: *El Amor Brujo* Milhaud: *Les Choëphores* Ives: *Concord Sonata*	Chirico, Carrà: *pittura metafisica* Nolde: 'The Burial'
1916	Debussy: Sonata for flute, viola and harp Ives: Fourth Symphony Prokofiev: Classical Symphony	Cabaret Voltaire, Zürich (Arp, Ball, Tzara) Joyce: *A Portrait of the Artist as a Young Man*
1917	Debussy: Sonata for violin and piano Satie: *Parade* (sets by Picasso) Ravel: *Le Tombeau de Couperin* Webern: Five Sacred Songs (1917–22) Busoni: *Turandot* Falla: *Three-cornered Hat* Stravinsky: *Les Noces* started, meets Picasso v. Moellendorf; quarter-tones	Freud: *Introductory Lectures on Psycho-analysis* De Stijl founded (Mondrian, Van Doesburg)

Year	Music	Other
1918	Stravinsky: *L'Histoire du soldat*, *Ragtime* Milhaud: *L'Homme et son désir* Debussy d.	Cocteau: *Le coq et l'harlequin* Apollinaire d. Proust: *À l'ombre des jeunes filles en fleurs*
1919	Bartók: *The Miraculous Mandarin* (first performed 1926) Satie: *Socrate* Milhaud: *Le Boeuf sur le toit* Hába: String Quartet (quarter-tone)	Bauhaus founded Trakl: *Dichtungen*
1920	Stravinsky: *Pulcinella*, *Les Six* formed Busoni: *junge Klassizität*	Modigliani d.
1921	Berg: *Wozzeck* Janáček: *Katya Kabanova* completed Milhaud: *Saudades do Brasil*	Picasso: 'The 3 Musicians' Kandinsky leaves Russia Mondrian: 'Painting No. 1'
1922	Stravinsky: *Mavra* Hindemith: *Das Marienleben*	Rilke: *Duino Elegies*, *Sonnets to Orpheus* Joyce: *Ulysses*
1923	Schoenberg: Five Piano Pieces Op. 23 (1921–3), *Serenade* Op. 24 (twelve-note technique) Stravinsky: *Les Noces* completed, Octet Strauss: *Intermezzo* Bartók: *Dance Suite* Kodály: *Psalmus Hungaricus* Janáček: *The Cunning Little Vixen* Hindemith: Sonatas	Chagall returns to Paris Braque, Picasso: still life paintings
1924	Schoenberg: Suite for Piano Op. 25, Wind Quintet Op. 26 Webern: Five Canons Op. 16, Three Folk Texts Op. 17 Janáček: *The Makropulos Affair* Fauré d., Busoni d., Puccini d. Nono b.	Th. Mann: *The Magic Mountain* A. Breton: First Surrealist manifesto Lorca: *Canciones*
1925	Berg: Chamber Concerto Webern: Three Songs Op. 18 Eisler: *Palmström Lieder* Janáček: *Sinfonietta* Shostakovich: First Symphony Schoenberg takes over Busoni's Berlin master-class Satie d., Boulez b.	Mondrian: *Die neue Gestaltung* Hofmannsthal: *Der Turm* Surrealist exhibition in Paris
1926	Schoenberg: Three Satires Berg: *Lyric Suite* Janáček: *Glagolithic Mass* Carrillo: micro-intervals Mager: Sphärophon Henze b.	First Klee exhibition in Paris
1927	Schoenberg: Suite Op. 29, Third String Quartet Op. 30 Stravinsky: *Oedipus Rex*	Picasso: monsters

Webern: String Trio Op. 20
Bartók: Third String Quartet
Křenek: *Jonny spielt auf*
Varèse: *Intégrales*

1928	Strauss: *Die ägyptische Helena*
	Schoenberg: *Variations for Orchestra*
	Webern: Symphony Op. 21
	Stravinsky: *Le Baiser de la fée,*
	    Apollon Musagète
	Bartók: Fourth String Quartet
	Janáček: *From the House of the Dead*
	Ravel: *Bolero*
	Messiaen: *Le Banquet céleste*
	Janáček d., Stockhausen b.
		Chagall: 'Cock and
		  Harlequin'
		Brecht-Weill: *Threepenny
		  Opera*

1929	Schoenberg: *Von Heute auf Morgen* Berg: *Der Wein* Hindemith: *Neues vom Tage*	Brecht-Hindemith: *Lehrstück* Hofmannsthal d.
1930	Stravinsky: *Symphony of Psalms* Webern: Quartet Op. 22 Dallapiccola: *Due Liriche*	Brecht-Weill: *Mahagonny* Brecht-Eisler: *Die Massnahme*

1931	Hindemith: *Das Unaufhörliche,*
	  Concertino for Trautonium
	Schoenberg: *Moses und Aron* started
	Varèse: *Ionisation*
	Messiaen: *Offrandes oubliées*
	Szymanowski: *Harnasie*
		Musil: *Der Mann ohne
		  Eigenschaften*, Part I
		Calder: mobiles
		Giacometti: sculpture-objects

1932	Schoenberg: Piano Pieces Op. 33	Broch: *Die Schlafwandler*
1933	Strauss: *Arabella* Hindemith: *Mathis der Maler* Bartók: Second Piano Concerto	
1934	Webern: Concerto Op. 24 Bartók: *Cantata Profana,* Fifth String Quartet Shostakovich: *Katerina Ismailova* Prokofiev returns to Russia	
1935	Berg: Violin Concerto, *Lulu* (unfinished) Webern: *Das Augenlicht* Gershwin: *Porgy and Bess* Jolivet: *Mana* Strauss: *Die schweigsame Frau* Prokofiev: *Romeo and Juliet*	
1936	Schoenberg: Violin Concerto Webern: Piano Variations Bartók: Music for Strings, Percussion and Celesta *La jeune France* formed	

1937	Schoenberg: Fourth String Quartet
	Bartók: Sonata for Two Pianos and
	  Percussion
	Stravinsky: *Dumbarton Oaks*
		Nazi exhibition of 'degenerate
		  art'
		Picasso: 'Guernica'

Shostakovich: Fifth Symphony
Dallapiccola: *Tre Laudi*
Hindemith: *Unterweisung im Tonsatz*
Ravel d., Szymanowski d.

1938	Schoenberg: *Kol Nidre* Webern: String Quartet Op. 28	

1939	Webern: Cantata Op. 29
	Tippett: Concerto for Double String
	    Orchestra
	Stravinsky, Hindemith emigrate to USA
		Joyce: *Finnegans Wake*
		Freud: *Moses and Mono-*
		    theism

1940	Stravinsky: Symphony in C Webern: Variations for Orchestra Messiaen: *Quatuor pour la fin du temps* Shostakovich: Piano Quintet Britten: *Seven Sonnets of Michelangelo* Copland: *Quiet City* Bartók, Milhaud emigrate to USA	Chirico: anti-modernism Klee d. Brecht: *The Good Woman of* *Szechuan*
1941	Dallapiccola: *Canti di prigionia* Schillinger: *The Schillinger System of* *Musical Composition*	Brecht: *Mother Courage*

1942	Schoenberg: Piano Concerto,
	    Ode to Napoleon
	Vogel: *Thyl Claes*
	Schillinger: *Mathematical Basis of the Arts*
	Messiaen: *Technique de mon langage*
	    musical
		Th. Mann: *Joseph and his*
		    Brothers

1943	Bartók: *Concerto for Orchestra* Dallapiccola: *Sex Carmina Alcaei* Britten: Serenade for Tenor, Horn and Strings	Brecht: *Galileo*
1944	Messiaen: *Harawi,* *Visions de l'Amen* Copland: *Appalachian Spring* Tippett: *A Child of Our Time*	
1945	Webern: Second Cantata Stravinsky: Symphony in Three Movements, *Ebony Concerto* Strauss: *Metamorphosen* Hindemith: *Symphonic Metamorphoses* *on a Theme by Weber* Britten: *Peter Grimes* Bartók d., Webern d.	Kandinsky d. Broch: *Der Tod des Vergil*
1946	Schoenberg: String Trio Elliott Carter: Piano Sonata	
1947	Stravinsky: *Mass, Orpheus* Schoenberg: *A Survivor from Warsaw* Hartmann: Fourth Symphony Cage: *Sonatas* and *Interludes*	
1948	Dallapiccola: *Il prigioniero* completed Messiaen: *Turangalîla* symphony	

Hindemith: *Das Marienleben* (revised version)
Boulez: Second Piano Sonata, *Le Soleil des Eaux*
Carter: Sonata for cello and piano
Schaeffer: first experiments in *musique concrète*

1949 Schoenberg: Fantasy for violin and piano
Prokofiev: Sixth Symphony
Messiaen: *Études de rhythmes, Neumes rhythmiques*
Britten: *Spring Symphony*
Strauss d.

1950 Schoenberg: *Modern Psalms* (unfinished)
Messiaen: *Mode de valeurs et d'intensités*
Cologne electronic studio established

1951 Stravinsky: *The Rake's Progress*
Hindemith: *Harmonie der Welt*
Boulez: *Polyphonie X*
Henze: *Boulevard Solitude*
Britten: *Billy Budd*
Messiaen: *Livre d'orgue*
Carter: First String Quartet
Cage: Music for Piano 1
Schoenberg d.

1952 Stravinsky: *Cantata, Septet*
Messiaen: *Timbres-Durées*
Boulez: *Structures* (first set)
Barraqué: Piano Sonata
Stockhausen: Kontra-Punkte (revised 1962)
Schaeffer: *À la recherche d'une musique concrète*

1953 Shostakovich: *Tenth Symphony*
Schaeffer: *Orphée*
Nono: *Epitaffio per F.Garcia Lorca*
Electronic works by Beyer, Eimert and Stockhausen

1954 Stravinsky: *In Memoriam Dylan Thomas*
Boulez: *Le Marteau sans maître* (revised 1957)
Varèse: *Deserts*
Copland: *The Tender Land*
Britten: *The Turn of the Screw*
Stockhausen: *Studie* II

1955 Barraqué: *Séquence* (1950–5)
Fortner: *The Creation*
Xenakis: *Metastasis*
Dallapiccola: *Canti di liberazione*

1956 Stravinsky: *Canticum Sacrum*
Nono: *Canto sospeso*
Henze: *König Hirsch, Maratona di Danza, Undine*
Křenek: *Spiritus Intelligentiae Sanctus*
Messiaen: *Oiseaux exotiques*
Stockhausen: *Gesang der Jünglinge,
Zeitmasse, Klavierstück* XI

1957 Stravinsky: *Agon*
Boulez: Third Piano Sonata, *Doubles*

Messiaen: *Premier catalogue des oiseaux*
Stockhausen: *Gruppen*
Henze: *Nachtstücke und Arien*
Xenakis: *Diamorphosen*
Suite for string quartet composed by Illiac computer

1958   Stravinsky: *Threni*
Boulez: *Improvisations sur Mallarmé, Poésie pour pouvoir*
Cage: *Aria*
Vogel: *Arpiade*
Lutoslawski: *Funeral Music*

1959   Stockhausen: *Refrain, Zyklus*
Stravinsky: Movements for Piano and Orchestra
Carter: Second String Quartet
Britten: *Noye's Fludde*
Ligeti: *Apparitions*

1960   Nono: *Intolleranza*
Boulez: *Pli selon pli*
Stockhausen: *Kontakte*
Henze: *Der Prinz von Homburg*
Blacher: *Rosamunde Floris*
Cage: *Theater Piece*
Penderecki: *Anaklasis*

1961   Henze: *Elegy for Young Lovers*
Britten: *A Midsummer-Night's Dream*
Stockhausen: *Originale*
Carter: Double Concerto for Harpsichord and Piano with Two Chamber
    Orchestras
Berio: *Circles*

1962   Stravinsky: *A Sermon, a Narrative and a Prayer*
Stockhausen: *Momente*
Kagel: *Sur scène*
Britten: *War Requiem*
Tippett: *King Priam*

1963   Stravinsky: *The Flood*
Henze: *Novae de infinito laudes*
Lutoslawski: *Trois poèmes d'Henri Michaux*
Penderecki: *Canon, St Luke Passion*

1964   Halffter: *Espejos*

1965   Henze: *Der junge Lord*

1966   Stockhausen: *Telemusik*
Henze: *Die Bassariden*
Barraqué: *Chant après chant*